Sacred
STRESS

A Radically Different Approach to Using Life's Challenges for Positive Change

George R. Faller, MS, LMFT
and The Rev. Dr. Heather Wright

Walking Together, Finding the Way®
SKYLIGHT PATHS®
PUBLISHING
Nashville, Tennessee

Sacred Stress:
A Radically Different Approach to Using Life's Challenges for Positive Change

2016 Quality Paperback Edition

Library of Congress Cataloging-in-Publication Data

Names: Faller, George R., 1970– author. | Wright, Heather, author.
Title: Sacred stress : a radically different approach to using life's
    challenges for positive change / George R. Faller, MS, LMFT, and The Rev.
    Dr. Heather Wright.
Description: Woodstock, VT : SkyLight Paths Publishing, 2016. | Includes
    bibliographical references.
Identifiers: LCCN 2016001161| ISBN 9781594736148 (pbk.) | ISBN 9781594736247
    (ebook)
Subjects: LCSH: Mental health—Religious aspects. | Stress
    management—Religious aspects. | Stress (Psychology)—Religious aspects.
Classification: LCC BL65.M45 F35 2016 | DDC 204/.42—dc23
LC record available at http://lccn.loc.gov/2016001161

ISBN 978-1-68336-275-3 (hc)

10 9 8 7 6 5 4 3 2

Manufactured in the United States of America
Cover and interior design: Tim Holtz
Cover art: © f9photos/Shutterstock

SkyLight Paths Publishing is creating a place where people of different spiritual traditions come together for challenge and inspiration, a place where we can help each other understand the mystery that lies at the heart of our existence.

SkyLight Paths sees both believers and seekers as a community that increasingly transcends traditional boundaries of religion and denomination—people wanting to learn from each other, *walking together, finding the way.*

SkyLight Paths, "Walking Together, Finding the Way" and colophon are trademarks of LongHill Partners, Inc., registered in the U.S. Patent and Trademark Office.

Walking Together, Finding the Way
Published by SkyLight Paths Publishing
A Division of LongHill Partners, Inc.
An Imprint of Turner Publishing Company
4507 Charlotte Avenue, Suite 100
Nashville, TN 37209
Tel: (615) 255-2665
www.skylightpaths.com

Contents

PROLOGUE

Our Stories

Encountering My True Self

GEORGE

On September 11, 2001, the New York City Fire Department (FDNY) lost 343 members, the largest loss of life of any emergency response agency in history.[1] In one brief moment, the world turned upside down, throwing most firefighters headfirst into a raging ocean of chaos and distress. Shortly after the first plane struck the North Tower of the World Trade Center, I left my home and my crying wife, Kathy, as she was holding our newborn son, and reported to Ground Zero. As a New York City firefighter, I could not stop to comfort her; I had a duty to fulfill. Worrying was not an option. I had to trust my training, get into survivor mode, and concentrate on the mission of rescue and recovery, not knowing which of my friends were dead and missing. Burned into my memory is the disarray I encountered right after the second tower collapsed, a scene of surreal devastation unlike anything I had ever seen before. The twisted steel, smoke, dust, eerie silence, and frightened faces jumbled together into a real-time nightmare. My impulse was to flee, but I chose to go forward.

The first day was a blur as I fought to suppress a multitude of feelings—frustration while I waited to do something, helplessness when I finally was able to search but found nothing, sadness for the emerging long list of lost friends, anger toward the attackers, and fear about what could happen next. On September 12, I was part of a team searching for victims and remains in the burning debris deep inside Ground Zero. Our task was to squeeze into voids created by the collapse, working in limited visibility due to the smoke, and try to find bodies, alive or dead. All rescue workers were informed that if we heard a loud gonging sound, it was a warning signal that the damaged adjoining buildings might collapse and firefighters engaging in search operations needed to find safe shelter away from the collapse zone.

My team and I had just discovered a cavernous void within the twisted steel when we heard unmistakable gonging. I will never forget the panic that arose in my chest when I thought about being buried alive and never seeing my family again. I remember thinking I didn't even have a radio to call for help, and it would probably take weeks for other rescuers to find my body. Fighting the urge to run, I also realized that someone might be alive just a few feet away from me. I knew if I left I would be breaking my oath to give my all to rescue a victim or fallen brother. Our team decided we were safely below the collapse zone, although in truth we didn't really know where we were. We recognized this might be our only chance to find survivors, and if roles were reversed, we would expect other firefighters to push ahead and try to find us. So we ignored the gong, put fears aside, and pressed on with the search.

I am so thankful for my training to turn off my fears during a crisis and focus on the tasks at hand. In life-and-death situations, the ability to stay calm under pressure is incredibly adaptive. Our society values steady performance during times of stress. No one wants his doctor before surgery expressing her doubts and insecurities, or a firefighter talking about being scared while heading toward a fire. Short doses of managing stress by suppressing emotional signals are sometimes absolutely necessary.

Nevertheless, managing stress with habitual emotional avoidance exacts high costs. Chronically disregarding the emotional signals accompanying stress leads to imprecision and lack of awareness. When someone doesn't listen to his inner world, he doesn't develop words to articulate his experience. When a child cries and no parent responds, the child learns to stop crying. As the child grows she continues to feel sadness, but the ability to express sadness is compromised. Over time the unused muscles wither, and crying is no longer a viable option. As an adult, her ability to express sadness takes on a vague and nameless quality. The emotional signals are still internally active, but the individual is not tuned into the frequency.

Those who study stress have found that long-term emotional numbing leads to a sense of self that lacks coherence, continuity, clarity, and comprehensiveness.[2] No wonder I was so confused in the days after September 11. I had stopped listening to the messages my body was trying to tell me. Disregarding the wisdom of my emotions made me susceptible to the negative impacts of stress—sleeplessness, loss of appetite, moodiness, and an inability to concentrate. Not listening to my distress signals of helplessness and sadness, which were pleading for me to reach toward comfort and connection, left me utterly alone to face unrelenting stress. When I returned home exhausted on September 13, I did not tell Kathy about my experiences in the previous days, nor did I have the energy to ask about hers. She already had too much to worry about, and I could not add more to her plate. I shielded her and our relationship by further burying my emotions. There is a saying proudly displayed in every firehouse: "Everything you see here stays here"—and I followed all the rules I had learned about separating family from work.

Over the ensuing months after 9/11, I was unable to share with Kathy the horrible things I was seeing or the risks I needed to take. Working day and night, I moved from the rescue and recovery effort at Ground Zero to the survival effort at home, "protecting" my wife by keeping inside the awful realities I witnessed every day. I hid my powerful feelings of anger, sadness, shame, fear, and helplessness. Kathy adopted a similar coping strategy. Realizing I was overwhelmed, she did a noble job of sheltering me and soothing her own feelings—her fear and loneliness. She gave me space and learned to depend on herself, believing it was unfair to make demands on me when I was doing my best to help so many people. We were just trying to endure, but the emotional price was costly. At a time when we needed each other most, we were moving apart.

Our method of coping with stress was an amazing testimony to the strength of love and sacrifice, but because it was done through avoidance and suppression, it never had a chance of working for the long haul. Instead of reaching toward each other for healing support, we were growing apart. We were not alone in our drifting. Distant marriages became epidemic within the FDNY. The sad reality was most firefighters either didn't recognize the serious threat of this emotional distance, or they had no idea how to bridge the gap.

Like most firefighters, I found it easier to give to others than to take a hard look at myself and figure out what I needed to receive. I had no experience or muscle memory of asking for help, so predictably I didn't ask. Looking back, the saddest part wasn't the isolation, but the fact that I assumed my struggles were a result of something being wrong with me. Firefighters know being alone during a fire is not good, yet somehow we're supposed to handle the stress after a fire differently. How unfair not to be taught how to reach for support and then blame yourself for not knowing how to do it.

As the days ground on and I kept pushing, my stress increased as my personal well-being declined. I tried so hard to do the right thing, only to find myself in jeopardy of losing everything important to me. Though I had grown up in the church, I hadn't learned the strategies and perspectives that I needed to deal with the pressures I faced. Stuck alone with unrelenting stress, I watched my mental, emotional, physical, and spiritual essence deteriorate. I became more reactive and defensive. I was failing as a firefighter, a father, and a husband.

As my situation became increasingly bleak, I had an epiphany: the rules I had always relied on about denying the effects of stress just did not work. Turning away from Kathy when we so urgently needed each other was crazy. By withholding ourselves out of our desire to offer one another loving protection, we essentially barred any hope of receiving the responses we so desperately needed. My intuition urged me to escape from this deadly snare of seclusion. This time I listened to my internal emotional signal of helplessness and reversed course, heading home for some much-needed sustenance.

Kathy and I agreed to give up our strategy of mutual avoidance. I'll never forget the profound relief and reconciliation I experienced after Kathy was able to listen to my feelings of helplessness and fears of failure and just felt sad for me. She didn't know what to say, but her eyes let me know that she was with me and I was no longer alone. I let her into my secret world, and she jumped into the hole with me and gave me permission to face my negative feelings. Throughout our relationship, we had shared many happy moments together, but this was the first time we truly shared our insecurities and vulnerabilities. Being in the hole together meant we were no longer alone, and that makes a huge difference.

This watershed moment altered my perspective on dealing with stress. My wife and I discovered that sharing our stress offers amazing opportunities for vulnerability and connection. Acclaimed author and research professor Brené Brown's research convincingly argues that rarely does someone's attempt to fix a problem make anything better. What makes something better is the very act of connecting.[3]

As a parent I have tried to fix problems rather than focus on connection more often than I'd like to admit. I vividly remember my oldest son, CJ, coming off the bus after school one day animatedly telling me a story of how he got detention because the teacher thought he'd thrown a piece of paper in class when actually his friend had committed the offense. He said, "Can you believe it, Dad? Totally unfair!" He was looking for connection, for me to join him in his indignation at this betrayal of justice. Unfortunately, I missed his signal and used his sharing as an opportunity to lecture him on the benefits of standing up for himself. I tried to love him by giving advice on what to do differently, which shut him down quicker than taking the ALS ice bucket challenge. I missed a golden opportunity to connect with CJ because I couldn't resist my urge to fix the problem and protect him in the future. So often as parents we pester our kids to engage without realizing how our relentless attempts to help are driving them away.

Every event holds the potential to either enhance or disturb connection. Realizing that stress can provide a doorway into stronger bonds and more meaningful encounters empowers us to seize the opportunity. The tragedy of 9/11 provided my wife and me a portal into deeper intimacy. We replaced our typical attempts to find solutions to our problems, which usually resulted in more distance, with a simple focus on being present to and caring for the other person. In the loving presence of my wife, I encountered my true self.

I am convinced that the act of sharing vulnerability not only creates the richest environment to truly know oneself, but also offers a spiritual space where we can fuse with a source of love much bigger than either partner.

Sharing the Power of Vulnerability

The calamity of 9/11 and its aftermath presented me with the proverbial fork in the road. One path headed toward chaos, defensiveness, and despair, while the other led to redemption, connection, and growth. I am fortunate that I grasped the opportunity to find meaning in the madness and in the process tapped into God's passion for connection. Throughout the Bible, there are countless stories of Jesus helping with compassion and comfort—not giving advice, fixing problems, or criticizing. Following his lead, I also saw a chance to serve and help others who were struggling with traumatic stress.

Alongside my full-time job as a firefighter, I decided to volunteer my services on my days off as a counselor to assist in post-9/11 firehouse critical incident stress debriefings. Walking into a firehouse that lost fourteen members and trying get them to talk about their feelings was a pretty intimidating challenge. When visiting a firehouse, we never knew what responses waited for us inside those big red doors.

We encountered the whole gamut of emotions, from big smiles and laughter to tears, rage, and silence. I heard countless stories of families and marriages under tremendous stress. I was stunned at the sheer magnitude of my fellow firefighters' struggles with anxiety, depression, addiction, violence, and infidelity. September 11 shattered so many firefighters' worldviews and trust in people. Overnight, devoted family men threw caution away and adopted a new perspective: "Life is too short, so play hard." Their intense acting-out behaviors stood in stark contrast to the apathetic communication between firefighters and their family members. At a time when firefighters desperately needed others to support them in facing overwhelming amounts of stress, many didn't know how to seek and receive help and so were left alone to confront the darkness.

I felt a deep pressure to reduce the pain within firefighters' families, yet my attempts to find mental-health providers outside the FDNY to help bridge the growing distance in relationships fell short. Despite my training in graduate school, it never occurred to me that *I* might be a resource for firefighters. As a rule, firefighters tend not to share intimate information about their marriages with other firefighters, so I assumed they would never allow themselves to be vulnerable enough to talk with me about their pain. In fact, when I first decided to go back to school and become a therapist, I tried to hide it from my coworkers. But, as in most families, keeping secrets hidden is hard. I remember coming into work one day and finding my locker spray-painted with hearts and flowers. Sure enough, my fellow firefighters found out I was in school to become a marriage therapist, and they decided to rename me "Cupid." Not the most menacing of names in such a macho profession. I still smile remembering a fire where one of my buddies screamed at me, "Hey, Cupid, break down that damn door!"

As a peer counselor, I was a member of a coordinated mental-health team providing treatment. During a staff meeting of the FDNY Counseling Services Unit a few months after 9/11, I was confronted with a moral dilemma. Directors from different locations within the FDNY were reporting similar results—lots of therapists volunteering their time to help individual firefighters deal with their personal psychological issues and very few mental-health providers stepping forward to help couples and families. It seems many therapists are more comfortable seeing individuals rather than couples and families. There is something about lots of people fighting each other in a tiny therapy room that is much more intimidating than working with just one individual. I sat in the corner thinking to myself, "Wow, these reports are dreary, and firefighters really need help in their marriages, and I'm becoming a couples therapist. Maybe I should give it a shot." My greatest fear was that if I tried to help, I might be rejected and ostracized by my fellow firefighters. I fit in well at the firehouse, and I didn't want my peers to change their perception of me as a no-nonsense, take-care-of-business tough guy into that of a sensitive, in-touch-with-his-feelings therapist with questionable bravery. There was a lot to lose, and I was unsure if firefighters would risk letting me into their intimate world. I understood the firefighters' dilemma; they felt stuck and alone with nowhere to turn. They didn't trust outsiders, couldn't turn to other firefighters, and didn't know how to reach out to their spouses. Given the utter desperation, I decided therapy with me, a fellow firefighter, was a better alternative than no one at all. I hesitantly raised my hand to offer my services to the FDNY Counseling Services Unit.

I underwent a baptism by fire. Immediately, I went from a novice therapist to seeing eight couples a day. My fellow therapists often knocked on my therapy room door and asked if I could keep the noise level down, as my screaming couples were distracting their individual clients. I felt lost and overwhelmed. Imagine the stress of not knowing what you are doing while trying to appear the expert helping couples reconnect. In this time of great need, I met my mentor, Dr. Susan Johnson—founder of Emotionally Focused Therapy (EFT), a short-term, structured approach to couples therapy—who provided me with a road map for navigating the landscape of love relationships. Coupling EFT with my personal work on vulnerability with my wife, I started to see results. I believe the greatest gifts we can give to another person are our presence and our willingness to join with them in creating a safe space for exploration and discovery.

As I continued to sit with my couples in the atrocious aftermath of September 11, we discovered the horror was also a pathway toward transformation for those courageous enough to open the door. As I came to trust the incredible capacity of human connection to promote healing, I wanted to wield it as a powerful tool for therapeutic change. By tapping into the incredible energy of vulnerability, my sessions dramatically changed from screaming to crying and laughing. People noticed and wanted to know what kind of magic I was wielding behind closed doors.

Trusting stress and vulnerability as a vehicle for positive change shifted my life both professionally and personally. Instead of feeling the pressure of constantly pushing for results, my focus turned toward slowing down and opening up a safe place where I allowed myself to be pulled into another's experience. Like those who practice judo, I learned to go with the force of emotions instead of resisting them. Allowing myself to curiously lean into emotions was incredibly energizing compared with the deadening effect of avoiding emotional signals. As my energy increased, so did my therapeutic results, and my successes thrust me into a leadership position of a very important movement.

Well, God certainly has a funny sense of humor. If you had to pick an ambassador to spread a message about the importance of vulnerability and emotional connection, you would want someone with the right credentials—maybe an articulate Ivy League graduate or an inspirational peace activist or even a sensitive artist. Instead, God chose an emotionally constricted New York City firefighter of Irish descent who often mispronounces words and resists crying and expressing feelings. Growing up in a tough blue-collar New York City neighborhood, my idea of vulnerability was avoiding it at all costs. I believed in the traditional definition of vulnerability as a weakness that leaves one open to attack and defeat. No one I knew growing up was proud to be vulnerable. And at age twenty-two I found a job that rewarded my ability to emotionally shut down. Surely someone else would be better qualified to lead this movement.

I am constantly amazed and humbled when I share my experiences all around the world and receive feedback that my story inspires others to see new possibilities in dealing with trauma and adversity. The power of my story is how it taps into our universal need to embrace stress as God's sacred instrument to unleash the power of vulnerability and connection. Stress pushes for change. Without it we'd be self-reliant islands with no need for others. To be fully present and alive, we need to see the value in everything God creates, especially our failures and mistakes. "Be not afraid" is one of the most common statements in the Bible. I believe preventing fear from occurring is not the goal; rather, it is using fear to turn us toward our Maker. Stress is a relationship builder. Created in God's image, we reach a state of deep communion by sharing pain rather than trying to avoid it. If the best way to grow spiritually is often by getting it wrong rather than right, then stress is an amazing catalyst for fostering union and transformation.

Learning from the Unimaginable
HEATHER

What's the unimaginable for you? For me one unimaginable thing was getting divorced. I was a pastor, counselor, and spiritual director. I had performed weddings for many friends, written and preached about the sanctity of marriage, and counseled many couples in distress. I was confident, probably too much so, that divorce would never be my fate. I believed I had the tools to avoid having a marriage breakdown. I was wrong. My marriage failure, divorce, and then the years that followed have been the most painful and stressful part of my journey. However, I learned a great deal about myself, faith, and healing that I could not have any other way.

Suffering and stress do strange things for us. It's nearly impossible to appreciate the gifts that they bring to us until we have the perspective of time and distance. Let me tell you a little of my story, when I had to face my "unimaginable."

After graduating from Princeton Seminary, I had been on the road to professional and academic success. I had also undergone eight years of infertility, finally becoming pregnant and giving birth to my beautiful, precocious daughter Alyse. By the time Alyse was one, I found myself living in a beautiful home with sweeping views of Puget Sound and the Olympic Mountain peaks, owning a boat, teaching graduate students full-time with my spouse, and enjoying a growing career as an author. What could be more grounded? My life seemed full of blessings.

But soon the happy story came undone. My marriage ended. Despite all the shared struggles along the way, my husband and I reached an impasse that we were not equally committed to overcoming. My heart was shattered in a million tiny pieces, and I wasn't sure I could go on living. I had always feared my former spouse would die before me, and I would be left trying to make meaning out of my grief and loneliness. I had no idea I would be in my thirties when our marriage would end in a much more painful and devastating way. By the time my daughter was two and a half, I found myself on a plane with Alyse and my parents, flying back home to Connecticut.

I took my keychain out of my purse and stared at it for a long time. It was empty. I no longer had a car key; I had sold the car a few weeks before moving. I had left my job—so my work key was gone. The house was a few months from being sold, and that key was no longer on the chain. I had also turned in the keys for a large apartment Alyse and I had lived in for the past eight months. I was "keyless." It was a chilling moment. Yet by stripping away so much that gave my life definition and meaning, I discovered something far deeper and more precious than any material possession. I found the simple scriptural truth that God does not abandon the widow and orphan, the alien and stranger. They are welcomed in by those faithful to God's call to protect, care for, and love those in need. My young daughter and I had become, for a season, those people in need. We received grace and kindness many times over, nearly overwhelming blessings in the midst of the pain and loss.

I found I was on an amazing journey of faith, walking through the valley of the shadow of death, deep sorrow, humility, and grief. I found God waiting there along with so many friends and family who were obedient to the call to love, serve, and give of themselves on behalf of another. A new friend went out of her way to help move my belongings out of my home to my new apartment. On my first Mother's Day as a single mom, four friends came with flowers and bags of groceries and set about making meals and filling my freezer. Another friend came over to take my daughter for a walk to feed the ducks so I could have a little down time. The smile and caring response of a checkout clerk, the helpful credit card serviceperson on the phone, even strangers communicated grace to me during my darkest hours. Because we were uprooted, we were able to move across the country so that my daughter could be raised surrounded by my loving extended family. Doors opened and ways were made clear that felt miraculous and surprising.

I had heard it said, "Be kind; you never know what someone else is going through." Suddenly, I found myself that "someone else" in need of a gentle touch and thoughtful response. When we are busy and preoccupied and things seem to be going our way, we can miss out on experiencing gratitude and compassion. It is in our most raw and vulnerable states that we have the opportunity to see the world around us and even ourselves differently. Perhaps you have had the same experience. I believe that when we endure seasons like this in life, we are more grateful for the kindness received and become more able to offer it to others who are likewise struggling. I remember a sweet moment with one of my relatives who said, without any sarcasm, "Welcome to the club." She was referring to the courage it takes for those going through divorce to keep living and hoping in the face of life's defeats.

Homelessness, divorce, job loss, bereavement, transition—can any of these be a state of grace? I believe so. The downward spiral can sometimes help us clarify our perspective about what matters in life, who matters, how we want to live whatever time is left to us. After divorce, my plans for my "one wild and precious life" (as poet Mary Oliver would say) were different than anything I ever would have expected. I wanted to work three-quarter time, not full-time; I wanted to wear not ten hats, but two—chaplain and mom, in recovery. That was plenty to do and be.

Who I Am

In sorting through our values, and what and who matter most, it is important to reflect on where we have come from and where we are going. As I review the trajectory of my own career, I am aware that I have had the privilege of wearing a number of hats in caregiving work, from chaplain to counselor, professor to minister. Currently, I direct a nonprofit faith-based counseling center, see clients, speak, and write. In each role, I have tried to assist others in finding freedom, hope, and meaning.

When I consider my life story and the events that shaped me and set me on this course of caregiving, I recall a dream that I had at fifteen years of age. I didn't remember it until a decade later, while I was in graduate school, when I reviewed an old journal. I can't say that I was overly religious at fifteen, but I was involved in my local youth group at church and trying to decide if faith had any bearing on my life. Was religious faith relevant and real? In the midst of these questions, the dream came. In it, I was standing on a ledge and above me was a bright light, like rays of the sun shining down. In front of me was a deep, dark pit, crowded with people. I could only see their outstretched hands reaching upward. I was bending over, offering my hand to pull others up out of the pit and move them toward the light. The dream seemed powerful to me and was filled with a sense of a divine calling. In many respects, the rest of my life has been a journey to discover the meaning of this dream for me and for others I encounter.

Helping others move from darkness to light has been an appropriate metaphor for my work in emergency rooms and nursing homes, along with counseling offices and in the pulpit. In many cases, I have been invited to listen and to share in intimate parts of people's stories. I have seen people rediscover life, find their smile, restore their lost sense of hope, and experience peace in the face of death.

As I have walked with others, I have confirmed this truth: each of us needs another person to be with us in the challenges life brings. Our cultural myth that we can handle life in isolation and we don't need one another to get along has been countered by both neuroscience and experience. Studies show that we are built for connection and relationship and become sick and depressed without them. The challenge is that we have to risk getting hurt and being rejected (for some that means repeating pain from the past) to find true community. We also benefit from finding relationships where we can be transparent and real about how we are doing. That is what I have seen as I have come alongside people who are struggling. Their pain strips them of masks, and they risk being honest about how they really are. As their counselor, professor, and chaplain, I have been honored to listen to them tell the truth about their lives. Their stories become a sacred trust to which I am called to bear witness. In many cases, people open up to me and then have the courage to also open up to trusted others in their lives. Their relationships often are then transformed and deepened. Journeying with others is humbling and both an honor and a privilege.

As I listen to their stories, I pray to discern the ways in which God is at work to bring hope, healing, and restoration. Each interaction has been like an archaeological dig, where there is a treasure to uncover if we only use the right tools and figure out where to excavate. Time and again, it is not about my words, skills, or technique, but rather the power of presence, my being in the moment with a person and focusing on his needs and hopes. When we are together in those difficult moments, something shifts for both of us. There are times we leave changed as a result of having known one another and walking a part of life's path together. For me, the stories of these people have brought me courage, helped me find my own tears, and emboldened me to live life to the fullest.

Why I Am Passionate about This Topic

Given my counseling and ministry of coming alongside others in their transitions and struggles, I have discovered that understanding the intersection of stress and spirituality is central to my life and vocation. Not only do I help my clients and staff manage their own stress, but I have plenty of my own to sort through each day.

From my own and others' journeys, I have discovered that grace is found when we step out of the routine and the comfortable. When we are on the edge, in the trenches, on our first silent retreat, in the hospital, we finally allow some margins on the edges in which grace can get to us.

As a person of faith, eager to receive this grace, I try to cultivate good spiritual practices to find a needed rhythm and balance in my life. We'll take a look at some spiritual practices in the pages ahead. My life circumstances demand that I pay attention to my spiritual path and its effects on stress, even if I would rather deny how much stress I am under. Learning from those I serve, I know most of us experience a deep spiritual hunger and desire to find a way to better manage our lives and thrive, no matter what circumstances we face. George's and my desire is that you will be more empowered to step into your stress and find hope and healing there for you and those you love.

Introduction

You likely picked up this book because you or people you love are dealing with stress, and you want help to resolve it or remove it. In our work as therapists, we often listen to individuals, couples, and families who are challenged by the stress of their lives, relationships, jobs, unemployment, grief, and transitions. Our motivation for writing this book is to share the knowledge behind our successful treatment in the therapy room with those who don't have access to face-to-face meetings.

The potential damage stress can cause is colossal. Many people hear their doctors say to them or a family member: "If you can reduce the stress in your life, then this situation will improve." Stress can seem like an ever-present villain lurking in the shadows, waiting to jump out and wreak havoc in our lives.

We are here to tell you a different side to the story about stress. Stress is much more than something bad that we fear. It can be a hero that we embrace. Our premise is that stress itself carries the potential for *both* good and bad. We invite you on a journey to uncover how you are engaging stress and to develop the skills needed to enjoy its benefits.

To help guide you on this journey, we explore the internal dimensions of stress, stress in relationships, and stress that arises from external sources. Although there is a great deal of overlap and interplay between these areas, we believe these groupings offer the simplest framework for organizing our experience of stress. When we discuss internal stress, we are focusing on stress within our individual bodies. We want to help you understand how you process your thoughts and emotions in either limiting or transformational ways. After exploring stress as it impacts us personally, we then expand the frame to include our relationships with others, such as spouses and children. Finally, we move from relational to external stress—things that cause stress but are outside our control. Being able to recognize the source of our stress—whether from the inside, from relationships, or from external factors in the world—empowers us to deal with it more constructively.

Our goal for you is to help you learn how to understand and navigate the stress in your life with more authenticity and integrity. Before we move into the content of our book, you deserve an introduction into what qualifies us as your guides on this journey. In the prologue, we presented our personal stories and why we are passionate about helping people deal with stress through new insights, healthier relationships, and deepened spirituality. In telling our own stories and those of clients we care for, we encourage you not to despair in the midst of your trials, but to find inner strength, faith, and community to support you as you survive and grow. Although stress universally impacts us all, each of us has our own unique vantage point on how we encounter stress. We believe a book on stress demands more than just one perspective.

As two very different people—George, a hands-on guy who loves telling stories, and Heather, who spent most of her adult years in graduate school and loves meaningful conversations—we hope to show varying ways of authentically embracing stress.

How Stress Works

Stress takes life and gives life. It is an inescapable part of our existence. Just like fire, stress holds the potential for both help and harm. It can propel us forward into new opportunities but can also hold us back in fear and exhaustion. The negative effects of stress are rampant. Our society is overworked and overwhelmed. When we are overstressed, we go into survival mode, which means we are more self-focused, more guarded, and less open to new ideas and the voices of others. As negative thoughts and feelings increase, they harm our relationships and reduce the quality of our lives. Too many people deal with stress through unhealthy coping (drinking or drugs, eating, shopping, zoning out in front of TV, psychiatric medicine, affairs, and so forth), which causes more stress, which creates a greater need for unhealthy coping. Everywhere you look, people are suffering the effects of chronic stress.

The costs of stress are immense. Research consistently reveals the negative physical impact of being "stressed out." The medical community cites stress as a major factor in almost every illness and disorder. Overall health, as well as the health of every system in our body—nervous, musculoskeletal, respiratory, cardiovascular, endocrine, gastrointestinal, reproductive, and immune—are adversely affected by stress and anxiety.[1] According to one researcher, stress likely accounts for more than half of the country's health-care-related expenses, playing a major role in diseases such as asthma, depression, migraines, heart attacks, cancer, and diabetes.[2] None of this is news to most of us. We don't need scientific research to convince us of the harmful effects of stress.

We know that stress can result in negative self-talk, that automatic stream of thoughts running about in our minds commenting critically on our situation. Negative aspects of life get magnified while positive ones are ignored. Imagine interviewing for a job and getting turned down. How do we handle the rejection? We might tell ourselves, "I am a failure, and I will never get a job. No one wants me!" Such thinking further contributes to our distress as the knot in our stomach grows and we feel more agitated or depressed. Such a defeatist attitude also damages our possibilities for the next interview. As negativity gets generalized, it becomes easier and easier to blame ourselves for all that is wrong. Poor results confirm fears of inadequacy. More self-blame leads to more negative thoughts, creating an ever more pessimistic outlook.

Using fMRI (functional magnetic resonance imaging) machines, which track blood flow to measure brain activity, neuroscientists can see live images of what happens to the brain under stress. Predictably, they have observed that stress impairs performance and function.[3] It negatively narrows our focus and reinforces neural pathways that emphasize pessimism. Caught in the stress trap, negativity breeds more negativity.

So how can we change this negative feedback loop and its harmful effect on the brain? The first crucial step is noticing that our perception of stress has swung too far toward the negative side of the spectrum. Too many of us are unaware of our prevailing negative views of stress, and we never even consider challenging our assumptions. As a quick experiment, randomly ask three people how they are doing handling stress in their lives. We bet all three people will presume the stress you are inquiring about is negative.

It is in our best interests to expand our mental framework and bring an optimistic lens to our understanding of stress.

Expanding the Definition of Stress

Generally most members of our society are well informed about the harmful effects of excessive and chronic exposure to stress. Yet the conventional definition of stress as a state of anxiety caused by the problems and pressures in our lives is far too limited. Focusing solely on the adverse effects of stress misses its essential nature and leads many people to think *reducing* stress is the gold standard for handling it. A more comprehensive understanding of stress views it as a necessary ingredient for change and progress. Without the vital energy produced by stress, organisms fail to flourish.

Seventy-five years ago, our society had a more holistic view of stress. Hans Selye, an Austrian Canadian endocrinologist, is considered the father of stress research. Selye's 1974 book, *Stress without Distress*, identifies two components, *distress* and *eustress*.[4] Distress is a negative state in which a person is unable to adapt or cope with stress. Distress is what most of us think about when we hear the word *stress*. It is associated with being overwhelmed and stressed out. For excellent reasons, most of us try to avoid the harmful effects of distress.

The second type of stress is called *eustress* (pronounced YOU-stress). Eustress is a positive response people have to a stressor that enhances their life and their abilities. It is usually related to desirable outcomes and feelings of engagement, satisfaction, and hope. Eustress is the fuel for our achievement and accomplishments. Eustress is not an emotion but a generative tension that causes growth—and we often have positive emotional responses when we recognize that growth. Your greatest memories—stealing that first kiss, getting married, witnessing the birth of a child, winning a big game—all capture the amazing effects of eustress.

Every challenge we encounter has the potential to trigger distress, eustress, or both. How we interpret stressful situations is incredibly subjective, though. If we were to poll an audience during a thriller movie, we would probably discover some viewers in distress (experiencing negative bodily reactions), some in eustress (totally engaging in the adventure), and others somewhere in between. The good news is, if you are in a state of distress, it does not need to be chronic or long lasting. We can learn to transform distress into eustress by making sense of it, coping with the situation, developing strength and resilience, and seeing the opportunity to grow. Imagine, for example, that instead of turning to a bottle when we are stressed out, we turn to a friend. Maximizing eustress while minimizing the chronic effects of distress is the secret to living an abundant life. Unfortunately, most people know nothing about eustress or its vital role.

After 9/11, a fellow firefighter I (George) knew was spending all his time after work at the bar. One night I joined him for a drink to check on what was happening. After some small talk and a few beers, he shared his story of removing debris at WTC Ground Zero and the unexpected horror of finding his best friend's crushed, burned, and dismembered remains. We cried together, sharing our sadness and helplessness. Looking back, I am convinced our sharing of that stressful event became the impetus for a stronger connection between us. Perhaps coincidently, my friend stopped spending all his evenings at the bar.

Fortunately, experiences like 9/11 are rare (although they seem to be increasing). Nonetheless, we all experience stress even in the ordinary difficulties of daily life. In social polling about what Americans are most afraid of, public speaking often tops the list. As a minister and professor, I (Heather) have had to spend much of my time presenting to groups. When I was young, I was shy and introverted and couldn't imagine drawing attention to myself, let alone commanding the attention of a whole group. But the power of relationship, particularly with my English teacher in middle school, gave me the courage to take a risk and do something I never could have imagined doing. I spoke in front of my English class, reciting a scene from *The Adventures of Tom Sawyer*. I still vividly recall the precise moment when my intense fear (distress) turned into quiet confidence that I could do it (eustress). The class voted me on to the finals for public speaking, and then I won for my grade, speaking onstage in front of all the junior high students and teachers. When I reflect on that event, which set some of my future career trajectory in place, I most recall the warmth and support of my teacher, not my breathless anxiety.

Distress can be transformed into eustress when we have a support system to encourage us.

The growth caused by eustress makes life worth living, and learning to channel the positive effects of stress leads to further happiness and transformation. Yet when we fall into distress, that, too, can provide an opportunity for growth. Then we have the opportunity to reach out to others, be honest about our struggles, shift our distress to eustress, and discover that both the highs and the lows are useful and necessary.

All experiences offer the possibility for both success and failure. A chart developed by a team of psychologists demonstrates the relationship between stress and performance.[5] It shows how performance increases with stress—but only up to a point. Eustress is the middle, sweet spot of a normally distributed bell curve of stress. It is the good stuff we experience when we are engaged, meeting the challenge, and thriving.

An absence of stress results in apathy—boredom, lack of motivation, indifference, lethargy, and poor performance. Avoiding stress kills our growth. Our performance also plummets, though, when stress rises to the level of distress, the opposite extreme of apathy. We experience distress when the stress level exceeds our capacity to manage it effectively and the strain wears us down psychologically, mentally, and spiritually.[6]

Based on personal experience and our work as therapists, and drawing on decades of psychological research, we have come to see stress as healthy and positive. We have also identified two key strategies for turning apathy and distress into eustress.

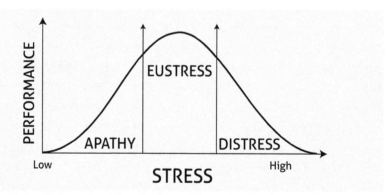

Hebbian Yerkes Dodson chart showing how different levels of stress affect our performance.

- *Reframing thinking*: The way we perceive stress matters. We can change how we think about pressures and problems, seeing them as opportunities for growth and transformation.

- *Embracing emotion*: We can use stress as a catalyst to lean into our emotions and share our vulnerabilities, strengthening connections and making space for even more positivity in our lives.

The illustration below shows these two paths. Reframing means consciously changing our brain's perception of stress. The second pathway requires going down into the heart, into the messy emotions caused by stress, listening to our underlying needs, and reaching out to others for support. It is our mission to help you learn how to adopt these strategies and turn stress into a positive force in your life.

According to our understanding, God's plan for stress is pretty straightforward. On so many levels—molecular, chemical, psychological, and spiritual—the operating system is the same: stress triggers a vulnerable reaction in adjusting to feedback that prompts us to reach toward another for help, which leads to connection and transformation. The apostle Paul writes, "Where sin increased, grace abounded all the more" (Rom. 5:20 NLT). If we were to replace the word *sin* with *stress*, where stress increases and we then turn to others and become part of something

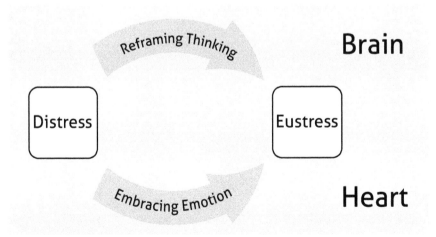

Two pathways for transforming distress into eustress.

bigger, grace abounds. How much fuller our lives can be if we accept the truth that as stress increases, it offers an opportunity for greater connections. Whether we experience distress or eustress, in the end both lead to deeper intimacy and awareness.

We believe God is the Great Recycler; everything God creates is purposeful and useful. God works with all of it, both the positive and the negative, with eustress or distress. If stress is the pressure that shapes our lives, then the good news is we are empowered to co-create and choose our path. Choosing to expansively reframe our thinking and to embrace the wisdom of our emotions is a surefire way to use stress to our advantage. Although everyone else may see stress as negative, we know the truth in our bodies: stress is a blessing that opens the door toward greater love and fellowship.

Part 1

How Stress Affects Our Interior World

Stress comes in many different forms and originates from a variety of sources. It can arise from external factors, such as economic failures or traumatic events. Stress can also result from challenges in our relationships with others, such as in marriage, parenting, and sex. Or it can come as a natural by-product of our own internal experience. Anger, fear, negative thinking, shame, and guilt are often examples of self-induced stress.

Typically, external, relational, and internal stresses all feed each other. As an example, an event like losing your job certainly can exacerbate tensions in a marriage, which in turn negatively impacts how you feel about yourself. Together, these three forms of distress can form a vicious feedback loop, with each increasing susceptibility to other types of distress.

After 9/11, the other firefighters and I (George) believed another terrorist attack was imminent. The external stresses of working at Ground Zero trying to find the remains of our friends while waiting for another attack

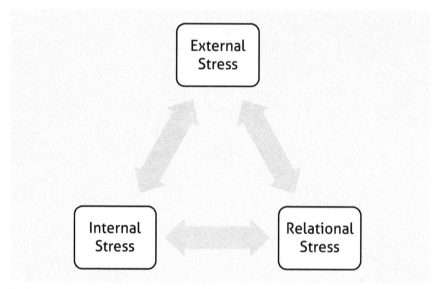

Trying to outrun stress in one area only increases it in others.

were intense. Not knowing how to talk about the pressures, helplessness and fears with colleagues or family members created distance in relationships. Mistrust in relationships caused isolation and internal self-doubt. Firefighters retreated into their individual worlds to gain a sense of control and order to the chaos. Alone, their doubts and uncertainties amplified. Insecurities led to more fear around external stresses. The stress-trap feedback loop picked up momentum as each stressor reinforced another. The cumulative effect was often too much to handle. Without help, too many first responders turned to coping with the stress by trying to escape through drinking, cheating, and fighting. Broken careers, marriages, and families were the by-product of poorly handled stress.

Many returning military veterans are experiencing similar fates today. In our experience of counseling veterans, the ultimate escape, suicide, feels for some like the only viable path for dealing with their pain. Returning veterans have a 50 percent higher suicide rate than the general population.[7] Our military deserves to know there are healthier ways to handle stress.

We believe the best starting point for understanding stress is by examining how stress impacts the individual's interior world. Internal stress has to do with how we process and interpret what is happening in, around, and to us. It is a function of both mind and heart. In order to enhance our ability to manage internal responses to stress, we want to repeat the two key moves we can make: (1) reframing our thinking about stress, and (2) learning to effectively connect to, process, and embrace our emotions about stress. Let's start by looking at some choices we can make in our thinking.

CHAPTER 1

Reframing Thinking

Expanding Our Perspective

According to Stanford psychologist Kelly McGonigal, "Science is proving that if you change your mind about stress, you can change your body's response to stress."[1] Viewing stressful situations as healthy and an opportunity for growth usually eliminates negative stress-related symptoms.

The power of optimism to positively impact our lives is well researched. Studies of survivors of SCUD missile attacks in Israel during the Persian Gulf War found pessimism led to increased anxiety and depression, while optimism reduced both.[2] After 9/11, I (George) certainly witnessed similar results. As unbelievable as this might seem, the terrible events of 9/11 still held the potential for eustress. Firefighters who adapted their lives to incorporate positive perspectives showed significant improvement. They used 9/11 to help them simplify their lives and put things in proper perspective. Every day they practiced appreciating their blessings, including their families, friends, God, and their health. Knowing the fragility of life, they did their best to "live life to the fullest." Unfortunately, other firefighters went in the opposite direction. They focused on losses, fears, and negativity. As they were consumed with darkness, their world shrank, and they desperately turned toward overworking, partying, and lashing out to escape their pain. Their lives unraveled as distress took its vicious toll.

A Harvard University study found that when participants were able to reframe a stressful event as a challenge instead of a threat, they felt energized when reflecting on the event and performed better than a control group who viewed the stress as negative. Even more interesting was that as the heart rate of the positive-stress participants increased to meet the challenge, their blood vessels stayed relaxed instead of constricting, the typical response to distress.[3] The same stimulus can cause two different physiological outcomes. Clearly our definition of stress really matters. Finding the right balance—allowing stress to sharpen our focus while not damaging our bodies—is a credible goal.

We can all practice moving our thoughts in positive directions. Some of us already achieve this shift through everyday activities like exercising. Although waking up early to hit the gym is not fun, we know the effort is good for our health. Embracing the pain while pushing our muscles to the point of discomfort is how we gain strength and stamina. Imagine how different life could be if we applied these lessons to other areas. Getting into a disagreement isn't so scary when we realize that repairing it can make the relationship stronger. The fight actually can help. Losing a job is an opportunity for a new, more rewarding challenge.

Firefighters practice this reframing every workday. When the bell signals the firefighters on duty to respond to a fire, it is normal for them to be anxious about heading toward danger. Yet the majority of firefighters learn to replace their fear with excitement. Sure, there is a possibility of danger, but there is also a chance to save someone and perform your job well under pressure. On a physiological level, looking forward to a challenge is a very different experience from just trying to survive.

While we were in the pressure-packed process of writing this book with looming deadlines and not enough time to write, we constantly reminded ourselves of the privilege of touching readers' lives. Choosing to see the potential for growth can turn a stressful situation into eustress instead of distress. Abraham Lincoln understood this when he said, "We can complain because rose bushes have thorns, or rejoice because thorn bushes have roses."[4] Think about these two radically different positions: complaining leads to negativity and distress, while rejoicing creates joy and eustress. It is the same bush, but two totally different perceptions of reality.

All events are doorways into either transformation or despair. What is so sad about the many lives destroyed by distress is that most people don't realize they have options. They just endure the distress as best they can. But a simple way to empower our decision-making capability is to follow these three steps: (1) recognize you are experiencing stress, (2) name the stress, and (3) reframe it.

Knowing, Naming, and Reframing

Most of us aren't completely aware of all the stress constantly bombarding our lives. We take it for granted. So taking the time to notice something is happening is the first crucial step in choosing how to deal with stress. If we do not notice the stress, we cannot turn it into eustress. Unfortunately, detecting the signals from our body that we are experiencing stress is often easier said than done. We are so inundated with stress that we fail to notice the signs of mounting pressure, worry, or unease. Practicing mindfulness, which focuses our attention on the present moment, enhances our ability to catch stress as it is happening.

Once we notice the stress, the next step is to name it. Naming involves an honest accounting of how we feel and getting to the root emotion behind our initial response. Not taking the time to name the signal means we miss the opportunity to gain clarity about our experience. We take ownership and responsibility for these signs from the body when we organize them into words, which provide order, structure, and control. On a neurological level, naming an experience engages the thinking part of our brain, which helps to calm the emotional reactivity. Without the words, we are left with ambiguity, imprecision, and disarray.

Imagine you are late for a work presentation. You run to an elevator and ask the person inside to hold the door for you. But not only does he not hold the elevator, he pushes the close door button, effectively ensuring you miss the elevator. If you do not organize the resulting anger, it will likely spill over into the upcoming presentation, and you will telegraph your irritation to your audience. Instead if you name the anger and attach it to the underlying feelings—your indignation at the person in the elevator, feeling of helplessness, and fear of being late—then you have a chance to replace the anger with a more constructive emotion for the presentation.

Step three is reframing the stress, which means expanding your perspective to include positive potential. In the previous example, naming your disappointment in another person's unfortunate action—closing the door in your time of need—allows you to recommit to your value of doing the right thing despite the costs in similar circumstances. Knowing you would have held the door allows feelings of pride and satisfaction to emerge and replace the anger. This negative experience provides an opportunity for affirming what you like about yourself—a much more constructive mind-set with which to head into a presentation.

Insightful research on people in stressful situations, such as test taking and public speaking, concludes that naming our anxiety and then reframing it as excitement makes a huge difference in our ability to deal with the stress and thereby improve our performance.[5] Test anxiety is a factor for all of us, no matter our age. We are being asked to perform, prove ourselves worthy, and meet certain criteria to succeed in life. Few of us breeze into an exam exuding confidence and feeling immune to stress. Instead, our legs may feel shaky and our palms, sweaty. We may notice our stomach churning and find we are taking short, quick breaths. Our body is providing us with valuable information if we know how to read the signs. Remarkably, adding a simple word like *hopeful* to the feelings of nervousness—"I'm nervous, but I feel hopeful about this test"—can make a dramatic difference in the outcome.

Understanding that behind any initial stressful trigger lies the possibility for us to imagine and create a positive outcome is essential to escape the stress trap and find freedom. Developing a victor's mentality, believing we can thrive with stress, is radically different from a victim's perspective, one that settles for mere survival.

Continuing with our earlier example, even if the missed elevator results in a poor presentation because of unprocessed anger and frustration, there is still an opportunity for reframing. You could choose to feel like a failure, a victim. In contrast, as a victor, you might say, "I can see ways it wasn't my best effort. I have also learned that I want to leave extra time before my next presentation, so I won't risk another elevator issue, and rethink my own disappointment so it doesn't spill over later." Those two different reactions to the same stimuli show the potential for a victim to reframe the event into the perspective of a victor.

It seems the Buddha is right: "We are what we think." In the Christian Scriptures, Philippians 4:8 talks about the importance of what we set our mind on, "Finally, beloved, whatever is true, whatever is honorable, whatever is just, whatever is pure, whatever is pleasing, whatever is commendable, if there is any excellence and if there is anything worthy of praise, think about these things." Wisdom throughout the ages tells us that how we think is important. The law of attraction, "Like attracts like," is based upon the idea that people and their thoughts are both made from "pure energy" and that like energy attracts like energy.[6] This belief suggests that by focusing on negative thoughts, we can bring about negative results, and by focusing on positive thoughts, we can bring about positive results. If you are embracing the positive potential in a circumstance, you will generate more positive energy and attract positive energy from others. The same can be said about attracting negative energy. This simple truth can be illustrated in how you address someone when seeking assistance. If you are positive toward her when soliciting help with your concern, you are more likely to get her assistance than if you approach her with anger and frustration. The feeling you send out is often the feeling you receive in return.

How Reframing Works

Let's apply reframing to your experience of stress at work. When you come home from a long day, you can choose how you interpret your stress. The negative path would be to conclude you are overworked and exhausted. The positive option is to believe the hard work is necessary and that you are grateful for being challenged. By catching the negative thinking and interpretation as it is happening, you can choose which energy to feed and which path you take.

Understanding and learning to notice the underlying mechanics of stress can help us reframe it. Daniel Siegel, a professor of clinical psychiatry at the UCLA School of Medicine, has devised a hand model for describing how the brain works. I (George) described this model to my son Dylan in an effort to make him more aware of his emotions. With one hand open, all five fingers extended, take your thumb and fold it into your palm. This represents the more primitive part of the brain, which is responsible for basic functioning and processing emotions. Then fold the remaining four fingers over the thumb, forming a fist. These four fingers represent the frontal cortex, which is responsible for higher functions like thinking. Well, sometimes (often, in my house) a stressful event triggers a strong emotional response in the older part of the brain (thumb), which causes a family member's thumb to blow off the lid (the four fingers, the frontal cortex).[7]

A few evenings after I'd described this to Dylan, he was watching his favorite show and his brother changed the channel—causing Dylan to lose his cool. Lashing out by calling his brother a jerk resulted in an argument that the whole family joined in. My well-intentioned lecture about how the brain works didn't seem to have made much difference in promoting better behavior, and Dylan stormed out of the room. I thought this was just another example of tuning Dad out. Well, a week later I was coaching Dylan in a pressure-packed basketball game when the referee made a terrible call. I lost my composure. In fact, I'm embarrassed to say, I was jumping around screaming (certainly not healthy for my body). In the midst of my temper tantrum, I noticed Dylan holding up his fist and demonstrating the lid being blown off. Immediately, I started to laugh. Getting help to notice how I was handling my distress empowered me to do it differently. Thanks, Dylan.

Another tool for reframing is to adopt helpful attitudes about the source of our stress. As we write this chapter, I (Heather) am sitting in the hospital beside my sleeping husband, who has had a stroke. He thankfully sustained no permanent damage, but recovery has been a slow process. I am aware of two ways of thinking about my circumstances. The first option is to view it as frustrating, exhausting, and traumatic. The second is gratitude that my husband is getting the care he needs. His life was saved. I can leave the hospital and entrust him to the staff's care, go home and rest, care for my children, and keep up with what needs to be done for my workplace.

Reframing and Spirituality

Many factors contribute to our perspective on how to handle stress, including our cultural background, previous experiences, formative stories, and genetic inheritance, just to name a few. Another factor is the spiritual tradition we received from those who nurtured us or that we ourselves found along the way. You may not have given much thought to your spiritual life, but our spiritual self-definition can root us in something greater, which is important in shaping how we respond to life's joys and struggles. Whether we feel adrift and uncertain, viewing the universe as capricious and dangerous, or we think our existence has import and occupies a place in a larger story, will affect how we interpret life's challenges. A spiritual awareness can also help us to affirm that there is always good in the midst of bad. Reframing by adding God to our stress equation reduces our distress, helping us believe that although we may not know the reasons for our trials, there is Someone in charge who knows better.

Ultimately, we find great security in knowing God wisely makes the problem (distress) itself part of the solution (reframing), leading us to transformation and deeper connection.[8] Trusting that God will find a way for love to seep in and bring light into the darkness offers comfort to us all. Seeing strength instead of weakness, an opportunity rather than a problem, something healthy instead of harmful, allows stress to stretch us for the better. What a profound shift to recognize that stress can extend and enrich our lives.

CHAPTER 2

Creating Connections

Learning to Embrace Our Emotions

By reframing our thinking about stress, we can have fuller, richer lives. In the same way, embracing our emotions—what they are, what they are telling us, and what we can do about them—enables us to live with joy and purpose, to develop more authentic and grounded lives. This strategy is more difficult for most of us than reframing our thinking because we are not as familiar with our emotional life as with our thinking. Most of us expend tremendous amounts of energy trying to suppress, ignore, tune out, or numb what our emotions are telling us. The information our emotions provide can be life giving and restore a sense of balance and peace, however. We need to be willing to lean in and listen—and perhaps act differently as a result of what we learn.

How Emotions Work

Every emotion is a form of energy providing information and serves an important function. Without emotions life would be pretty boring. Through them, we experience a whole gamut of responses, from the positive of fun and excitement to the darkness of fear and sadness. We will explore some specific emotions further in chapter 3, but to understand how embracing emotions enables us to turn distress into eustress, we can look at emotions in general. All emotions tell us what is happening in the moment and what we need. They are simply a signal from the body telling us something has changed for good or bad and that we need to pay attention.

Neuroscientists have learned in the past three to four decades that our emotions arise out of the most primitive part of our brain and that they are produced incredibly rapidly. Emotions can't afford to be slow; informing our reaction time, in certain circumstances, may make the difference between life and death. James Gross, a scientist who studies emotions, discovered it takes one-tenth of a second for the brain to register and react to a stimulus.[1] So if you are walking in the woods with a friend and see a shadow move in the grass, it takes one-tenth of a second for your brain to register threat and show the fear in your face, sending an immediate message to your friend that something is wrong. It takes six-tenths of a second (still pretty fast) for the message to get to the frontal cortex (thinking part of the brain), where the brain determines the stimulus was just the shadow of leaves blowing in the wind, not a snake. The problem is the half-second lag time between the initial registration of a threat and the frontal cortex decision to disregard it.[2] When your friend whose brain reads the fear on your face in one-tenth of a second asks, "What's wrong?" and you say, "Nothing, everything's fine," you are sending a mixed message, because your face said there is a problem while your words are saying everything is fine. We tend to believe the emotion. Appreciating the speed and wisdom of our emotional signals is the key to honest and direct communication.

In truth, emotions are exquisitely intelligent, and it is illogical to disregard the information they are sharing. Emotion shapes and coordinates our experience and communicates our needs to ourselves and others. As *movere* (to move), the Latin root of the word *emotion*, suggests, strong feelings literally move us to approach or to avoid. Emotions are a great motivational force pushing us to action.

The problem is many of us don't understand what our emotions are trying to communicate or where they are trying to move us. Because emotions are not always easily understood or contained, people in many cultures mistrust emotions, viewing them as misleading, needing to be tamed or controlled. Many of us are raised to believe that maturity is about governing emotions and relying on our thinking. As a result emotions are often pathologized and viewed as something to be overcome, not embraced. Emotions are often labeled as weak, dramatic, irrational, and problematic. Many of us learn at a young age how to suppress our emotions. Even our parents' well-intentioned assistance can often discourage embracing emotions. I (George) was reminded of this truth when my son CJ got off the school bus one day in first grade. CJ seemed down and said his friend Joey no longer wanted to be his friend at school. I felt bad and immediately wanted to protect both of us from the negative feelings by fixing the problem. So I responded, "Don't worry about it. Joey is a jerk. Let's call up Bobby for a playdate."

My attempt to avoid CJ's sadness and my own feelings of hurt resulted in sending the subtle message to CJ that it is not OK to share these "softer" feelings. CJ was being trained early on to hide his true feelings and adopt a veneer of strength by "soldiering on." The gloomy reality is that if I consistently discourage expressing vulnerable feelings, CJ will learn to protect himself by concealing his inner truth, moving him another step away from knowing and being able to act on his own emotions. Turning away from or hiding our feelings guarantees we will be alone when we feel bad. Instead, we need to learn how to lean into the hurt so we can listen to what the emotion is signaling.

For CJ to express his feelings, he needs his dad (George) to model how to embrace his feelings. We have identified the following four-step process for learning how to embrace emotion: (1) recognize you are experiencing an emotion by paying attention to where you feel it in your body, (2) name the emotion to engage your cognitive brain and provide perspective, (3) figure out what the emotion is signaling and what you need, and (4) make a decision to act.

This process of engaging emotion incorporates the popular concept of mindfulness, which is about being totally open to the present moment. It is only in being authentic by receiving what is, and moving into and through it, that we can attain peace and clarity. Mindfulness is not escaping life but entering more deeply into it. We do not suppress, deny, minimize, project, or rationalize what we feel; rather, we receive what is and embrace the message.

Using this four-step process, let's look at how I repaired my relationship with my son CJ after a poorly timed suggestion that CJ not "worry about it." First, I identified the bad feeling in my stomach (step 1) as I realized my advice to call up another friend did not lift CJ's mood. Then I named the bad feeling in my stomach (step 2) as helplessness and sadness at seeing CJ's pain. It hurts to witness your child in pain. Putting a label on the bodily sensation of the bad feeling in his stomach engages my brain to join the process. Making the emotion conscious and explicit allows me to focus more intently on the emotional signal. The good news is if we listen to the emotional message, not only does it convey the problem, but also the solution of what we need. I recognized my sadness and helplessness was trying to get me to seek connection and offer comfort to CJ (step 3). As a kid, I also experienced the rejection of peers, and I faced the pain alone. My only option as a kid was to try to avoid the pain. No wonder I tried to do the same with CJ! Plugged into my vulnerable feelings, I decided (step 4) to empathize with CJ instead of encouraging him to avoid his feelings. This last step of taking action to meet the emotional need is radically different from the inertia of emotional avoidance. Many times we can't fix the source of the hurt, but we can choose to use the adversity to turn toward those we love.

Rather than dismissing CJ's feelings with advice, I said, "I'm sorry, son. I said to not worry about it. Of course you are worried. I know it feels bad when someone doesn't want to be your friend. It makes sense you feel sad, and I feel sad, too." These words give CJ permission to listen to his emotional signal of sadness and trust his dad to be alongside him in moments of insecurity. Interestingly, sharing the sadness creates connection, the best antidote to what hurts. Our countercultural message is that hiding emotions leads to the distress of facing hurt alone, while embracing emotions leads to the eustress of dealing with hurt together.

Embracing Emotions Leads to Vulnerability

Openness to embracing our emotions is crucial to being authentic and truly knowing ourselves. Emotional awareness empowers us to understand our needs and communicate these needs directly. Yet this willingness to expose ourselves emotionally is risky. At the heart of all emotional engagement lies vulnerability. Most people want to avoid vulnerability because of the possibility of painful rejection. They believe that to be vulnerable is to be weak, exposing them to disappointment and hurt. Avoiding vulnerability seems the safest course. The problem with this strategy is that in avoiding our vulnerability we must hide our true selves. By erecting a wall, presenting a false persona of strength, we relegate our insecurities and needs to the shadows. We imprison ourselves, needing protection so we do not get hurt, only to discover our protective tactics work too well, as they also keep out any comforting responses to our vulnerabilities. Walls do not discriminate.

The only way out of this prison is removing the wall and allowing ourselves to be vulnerable. We (George and Heather) believe that, like common misunderstandings of stress, the traditional definition of vulnerability as weakness is limiting. We think of vulnerability as the willingness to be real and honestly share ourselves, especially our emotions, dreams, desires, talents, fears, doubts, failures, and flaws. At its core, vulnerability reminds us of our universal longing and need for connection with others. We are incomplete alone and crave to become part of something bigger than ourselves. Remove vulnerability, and we lose our greatest asset to connection, our authenticity. The risk and uncertainty inherent in vulnerability makes it the perfect raw material from which to build genuine relationships. Embracing the emotional signal of our vulnerability allows every encounter to offer a fresh chance for mutual discovery.

Sociologist Brené Brown's research sheds light on why embracing our emotions is so integral to optimal living.[3] People who live "wholehearted" lives characterized by joy, purpose, meaning, love, resilience, belonging, and creativity share one prerequisite: a sense of worthiness.[4] That sense arises not from the right education or job or from success, fame, or fortune, but from what is really important and life giving: deep connections with other people.

How do we deepen our closest connections? For Brown, our ability to be vulnerable—to show ourselves truthfully, warts and all, thus allowing another person to communicate that our blemishes are OK—empowers us to thrive. When we invest so much of our energy into showing others only what we anticipate they wish to see, we lose ourselves by performing, perfecting, defending, pleasing, and proving.[5] Our sense of worth depends on our ability to be vulnerable. This is a profoundly counterintuitive message within our culture, but there are no shortcuts to a sense of worthiness. To like ourselves, we must embrace our emotions, show our true selves, and allow others to safely respond with affirmation.

I (Heather), after a year of trying to get pregnant, lost a child through miscarriage. With my pregnancy loss, I had to bury my dreams by saying good-bye to the child I would never comfort or cuddle. Still today, I sometimes find myself wondering what my baby girl's face would look like.

Many women have told me their miscarriages were the most profound losses they experienced, causing them to question God's goodness or existence. For me, the next seven years of trying to conceive were monthly battles with loss and bearing the heavy burden of keeping hope alive for a better outcome. Everything in me wanted to give up, but somehow, by God's grace, I kept trying. Infertility work can be a painful, roller-coaster ride of treatments, procedures, daily blood draws, drugs, and agonizing months of waiting for any positive news. Sometimes good news doesn't come, or at least not in the form we would hope. After an eight-year battle, I finally was able to conceive and gave birth to my vivacious daughter, who is now thirteen.

How did I cope with the months of tortured waiting, painful procedures, drug reactions, repeated losses, and the ongoing story of failure? I found it was being real (as sometimes only grief can make us) with those who could uphold me, listen lovingly, and act with mercy on my behalf. It was friends and family that reminded me God's face is one of love and not condemnation in the place of defeat.

As a New Englander, being honest about how I am feeling with others is not something that comes naturally or easily. I come from the culture of the Puritans and the stiff upper lip. I remember the day when I finally decided to share that I had suffered a recent miscarriage with my class of eighty graduate students in Colorado during my lecture on development and loss. I wasn't sure I could get through my story without crying. As my voice cracked and eyes filled with tears, their looks of compassion and comments of grace convinced me that I did just what I needed to do. How better to share the intimate agony of loss than to say, "Hey, I am in it right now, and it's breaking my heart. But I can tell people around me care, and I can receive their love and grace, and somehow that is enough." I felt incredibly exposed but also free as well to acknowledge the dark mantle that surrounded me.

Applying our four-step process to embracing emotion, I was able to acknowledge the physical pain in my heart and the constriction in my chest that expressed the extent of my hurt, sorrow, and even embarrassment that I had lost a child and struggled with infertility. First, I named the truth of the pain inside. When I listened to my pain rather than pushing it away, I heard my desperate need for comfort and compassion for my tears, so I decided to reach out for support, and in so doing, I moved toward healing and being known through being real and honest about my own suffering. Rather than judgment or ridicule, I found grace and kindness, which brought relief to my hurt. This paradigm has continued to be true throughout my ministry and career, when I am real in sermons, with families at the bedside of a dying patient, and in dialogue with my spouse or children. I still feel a pang of fear that comes with being vulnerable but then I am rewarded tenfold by the response.

Because we are created in God's image, relationships are the essence of our being. To have good relationships, we must embrace our emotions and vulnerability. Think about the relationship most of us have with God. When do we turn toward God the most? During good or hard times? It is our challenges that most compel us to reach out for relationship. In fact, the origin of the word *religion* comes from the Latin word *religio*, which means to bind together or to reattach. Helping us reconnect with God is the primary goal of any religion. Connection is the whole point of our being, while separation goes against the very makeup of all of existence.

Interestingly, many neuroscientists are joining theologians in believing "our nervous systems are constructed to be captured by the nervous systems of others."[6] Think of the image of a parent holding a baby, both looking deeply into each other's eyes, sending clear, direct messages of how important each is to the other. Strong, resonant communication is occurring without words. From cradle to grave, we need to connect with others, with another nervous system, to ground us and tell us who we are, and in this grounding, we find our best selves.

The power of human relationships to help us change is well illustrated in the stories we tell. The fairy tale of Cinderella is a great reminder of our interdependent nature and the universal truth that others help define how we see ourselves. The nasty stepsisters had Cinderella convinced she was insignificant and ugly. At the ball, her fairy godmother and the prince revealed Cinderella's true, beautiful self to her. Her surroundings didn't change her essence but certainly altered how she saw herself. Cinderella realized her inner truth with the help of others.[7] If the people around you believe you are worthless, it is hard to believe otherwise. We all need fairy godmothers and princes in our lives, and we can be those for others as well. Supported by the loving arms of others, we discover our deepest truths and resiliency.

Vulnerability Is the Birthplace of Resiliency

Resilience is the process of overcoming adversity and turning distress into eustress. Embracing our emotions is the key to opening the doorway of resilience. Stress triggers emotional reactions that provide the impetus toward either vulnerability and connection or further isolation and protection. Even though stress can function in different ways, it is the essential stimulus for seeking and finding growth. Regardless of the type of distress suffered, the people who survive best don't look to return to their former life; rather, they welcome the creation of a "new normal." They are realistic, aware of their distress, and still able to seek out opportunities to transform their experience into eustress. Esther Perel, a noted author and therapist, grew up in a community of Holocaust concentration camp survivors, and she discovered there were two groups of people: "Those who didn't die, and those who came back to life."[8] Those who didn't die survived with perpetual distress. "They lived tethered to the ground, afraid, untrusting," and waiting for the next bad thing to happen.[9] In an unsafe world where fear dominates, there is no room for fun and thriving. Focusing all their energy on avoiding fear, they never could outrun its shadow.

Perel observed, however, that those who came back to life learned that the best way to escape focusing on perils is to concentrate on finding purpose for living. These Holocaust survivors did not get lost in the distress. Instead, they used the distress as stimulation to find meaning and fulfillment. Fear was replaced by curiosity and exploration. They never forgot the horror, but they used it to motivate positive living. Through embracing their emotions, they gained greater clarity of their own resilience. Among those who have found hope in the midst of great fears and challenges were Margret and H. A. Rey, authors of the famous Curious George series. They were German Jews who escaped the Nazis on their bicycles and intentionally turned unimaginable distress into eustress, inspiring millions to celebrate life.

We hope our point is crystal clear. The best things in life—love, connection, empathy, comfort, compassion, vulnerability, and resilience—are not possible without embracing our emotions. Emotions remind us that what matters most is the space between things, people, and relationships, not the isolated entity.[10] Everything in the known universe, from molecules to solar systems is dependent on relationships. Our Western ideology of autonomy and independence is a myth. In truth we are all functioning parts of something much bigger than ourselves. Reality is communion.[11] If we listen, emotions constantly let us know about our need to connect. Our emotional signals provide accurate evaluations of where we are in the present moment. If we are communicating our needs directly and they are being responded to, then our emotions typically signal positive feelings of contentment. If our communication is indirect through camouflaging or suppressing our emotions, then the scrambled messages often signal distress, which is pleading for us to repair and find connection. Do you reading this book have the courage to embrace your own scary and confusing emotional messages? We hope our argument to embrace emotions is bolstering your resolve. As we make ourselves vulnerable in the present moment with whatever the signal is saying, we develop our ability to be flexible and adaptive—to be masters of sacred stress.

Emotions and Spirituality

Historically, religious traditions view emotions with similar mistrust as the general public. Some believe that emotions, equated with passions and temptation, are evidence of weakness and sin. Resisting our emotions is linked with righteousness. For some, the goal is to disregard and overcome the body's signals and aim for a perfect state of calmness. We believe this saintly image of perpetual peacefulness is misguided and unattainable. It sets us up for failure by trying to avoid the compelling messages of the emotions God created in us so we can be aware of our needs and take steps toward meeting them. Fortunately, people are as effective at stopping an emotion as they are preventing a sneeze.[11] Our bodies are going to communicate, even if we try not to listen to them.

Looking to the Christian Scriptures, we can look to the life of Christ for clues to a healthy emotional lifestyle. The gospel writers paint their portraits of Jesus using a kaleidoscope of brilliant "emotional" colors.

Jesus felt *compassion*; he was *angry, indignant,* and *consumed with zeal*; he was *troubled, greatly distressed, very sorrowful, depressed, deeply moved,* and *grieved*; he *sighed*; he *wept* and *sobbed*; he *groaned*; he was in *agony*; he was *surprised* and *amazed*; he *rejoiced very greatly* and was *full of joy*; he *greatly desired,* and he *loved.*[12] How many of us give ourselves permission to feel so deeply? For Christians, Jesus Christ is an example of what it means to be fully human and made in the image of God. Jesus was not afraid of his emotions. He lived them fully and in doing so modeled the importance of paying attention to what emotions have to tell us.

Emotions are not morally good or bad; rather, they are indicators that help us survive and thrive. Learning to pay attention to emotional signals allows us to adjust our actions and continue growing. When we embrace our emotions, we honor their sacred function and allow our mind, body, and soul to come together into one integrated whole. We believe one of the major goals of healthy spirituality is to help us all feel more at home in our body and with our emotions. God wants us to embrace emotions because in the present moment we can encounter him. God is waiting to connect with us now, not in clouds of the future. Make haste!

CHAPTER 3

Opening the Door to Transformation

Knowing and Naming Our Emotions

Because embracing our emotions is an essential skill for turning distress into eustress, we need to be familiar and comfortable with our feelings. As noted in chapter 2, however, many of us have been taught to mistrust or dismiss our emotions. Consequently, we have difficulty knowing and naming our emotions so that we can then embrace them.

Paul Ekman, a pioneer in studying emotions, suggests six basic emotions—four negative and two positive—are universally recognized through facial expressions, regardless of culture or language.[1] These are anger, sadness, fear, and disgust (negative emotions) and happiness and surprise (positive emotions). Like the primary colors red, yellow, and blue, from which all variations of color emerge, so these basic six emotions form the foundation from which arise the hundreds of emotional responses of our complex emotional world. In this chapter, we'll examine these emotions to help you understand and name them as you develop in your ability to embrace emotion.

The Wisdom of Dark Emotions

As we begin this chapter, we invite you to consider making a seismic shift in your thinking. We believe the negative emotions of anger, sadness, fear, shame, and guilt are not, in fact, negative. Miriam Greenspan, in her book, *Healing through the Dark Emotions: The Wisdom of Grief, Fear, and Despair,* says there is no such thing as negative emotions, only "unskillful ways of coping with emotions we can't bear."[2] Changing our perspective—no longer seeing these emotions as negative but actually respecting their wisdom and redemptive nature—is essential to being able to manage stress effectively.

Anger

Anger is a natural response when something is wrong. Such things as a simple slight, an unpleasant event, an unfair action, a rejection, or a serious danger can trigger anger. It is an emotion that mobilizes the body to take corrective action, empowering us to stand up for our needs and say, "I am important and worthy of being heard."

It is in our best interests and of those we love to learn how to understand and engage anger well. Poorly managed anger is related to a slew of health conditions, such as headaches, sleep problems, fatigue, infection, digestive disorders, heart disease, and stroke.[3] If anger flourishes unchecked, it can lead to hatred and violence. In counseling couples, we have both witnessed how anger crushes intimacy, breeds defensiveness and distance in relationships, and breaks up families. Anger is such a universal danger that it was included by the early spiritual writers as one of the seven deadly sins.

Many of us think our best strategy for dealing with anger is to avoid it. We invest so much energy in repressing this emotional signal because we believe our relationships and the world in general are better without anger.

Surprisingly, anger can actually be a constructive and creative force. Research overwhelmingly indicates that feeling angry increases optimism and creativity and helps us perform more effectively. Expressing anger leads to more successful negotiations and mobilizes people into becoming agents of change.[4]

Anger also provides a sense of control against feelings of helplessness as well as confidence that the outcome can be altered. One researcher examined Americans' reactions to the terrorist attacks of 9/11 and found that feelings of anger helped minimize paralyzing fear, allowing people to come together for a common cause. Those who became angry were less likely to be afraid of future attacks.[5]

Many professionals, such as firefighters, police officers, and military personnel, are trained to use anger to push past their fears. Thinking about the terrible atrocities your enemy might commit to your friends and family provides extra energy to charge up a hill against machine-gun fire.

The feeling of anger isn't the problem; it's what we do with it that makes all the difference. The key is figuring out what need our anger is trying to communicate. Once we realize that anger is just asserting our needs, it gets easier for us to be more direct about communicating them.

I (George) remember trying to reach a customer service representative and getting redirected far too many times to automated voices. Each time I was put on hold and then asked to hit buttons, nothing worked. As my frustration mounted I kept pushing zero, hoping to speak with an operator, and then I was put back on hold for another half hour. By the time an actual live human person got on the phone, I was livid. I started screaming about not knowing how their company stayed in business with such terrible customer service. My anger was clearly communicating my need for the injustice to be acknowledged. Astoundingly, the lady on the other end gave me permission for my anger and said their company's response was unacceptable. After apologizing, she said she would do whatever was necessary to make the situation right. My signal (anger) about the unfairness of the treatment and my needing someone to listen was met; I no longer needed to send the signal (anger). It served its purpose and dissipated. Her interaction illustrates the power of someone understanding the need that anger is expressing. Imagine if instead of giving me permission to be angry, the agent had told me in the heat of my protest to calm down and stop being so difficult. My anger would certainly have increased.

Anger is powerful; it is very effective in getting responses. In couples and family counseling, we often find that it takes at least one partner's anger to bring awareness of what is wrong so the couple can find solutions. Anger empowers those involved to mobilize, in positive ways, to repair the relationship and get back a sense of harmony and reconnection. Take away our anger and ironically we lose the ability to fight for better relationships. Couples need anger to reach toward each other instead of going away. Although it is often lost in the intensity of the delivery, hope for change is the motivation behind anger.

We try to help couples approach their partners not only with different words and behaviors but also with an altered tone and mood. For example, a wife asking her husband in an angry tone, "Why were you so late getting home from work today?" expresses too much anger and no vulnerability. The husband will probably react with defensiveness and withdraw, which will only reinforce the wife's underlying fears of rejection. If the wife instead listens to her anger and discovers the need it is communicating, she might say in a softer voice, "Please listen. I get concerned when I don't know where you go after work. I feel like you don't want to be with me, that I'm not attractive to you anymore. Is that true?" This question will likely elicit a completely different response. It encourages the husband to engage and comfort her vulnerability, helping her get what she longs for. She is courageous and tells him what is really going on rather than leading with a verbal punch.

Although misplaced anger can be unhealthy in relationships, appropriate anger can offer a pathway toward healthier connection. The crucial factor is using anger constructively. Stepping back from a situation that has upset us gives us a chance to calm down and figure out what is disturbing us and what options for change we have.

Respecting the vital function of anger to get us moving honors its basic function: to create change. Anger protects us from worry, anxiety, and feeling powerless. Anger isn't a sign of failure; instead, it can be a catalyst for success. If we heed its advice, our lives are enriched.

Sadness

Sadness usually means something bad has happened; we have lost something or someone important, or we have failed at an endeavor. Sadness is a type of emotional pain and comes to all of us, no matter our age and in response to all kinds of losses. A wife whose husband dies after fifty years of marriage or a child who drops her ice-cream cone will both express loss.

Feeling down is a normal reaction to life's struggles. If the feeling is persistent, however, then it may be indicative of depression. Depression, unlike sadness, doesn't depend on circumstances. Depression is like a low-grade virus that causes general fatigue, discomfort, unease, slower thought processing, lack of interest in usual activities, lack of appetite, and excessive sleeping or inability to sleep.[6] Feeling sad isn't the primary problem of depression; rather, it is a lack of energy that makes depression so debilitating. Because expressing sadness uses a lot of energy and the body cannot maintain this expenditure perpetually, some people facing loss choose to shut down rather than stay present to the sorrow. Although this technique dulls the hurt, it also dampens all the other emotions as well. It is hard to feel happy and alive when you are numb. The negative impact of depression today is enormous. Depression is predicted to be the greatest single cause of diminished human potential in the near future, surpassing all other illnesses, including cancer and heart disease.[7]

Given the potential severity of depression, it makes sense that people want to get out of their sadness as quickly as possible. They are afraid that their sadness will lead to depression. Keeping busy is a great strategy to ensure there is no time for sadness. Yet trying to avoid feeling sad guarantees that we will miss the wisdom of the signal. Sadness is communicating that something important is happening and we need to pay attention. If we open our hearts to listen to what sadness is saying, then we can learn about its amazing benefits.

On a physical level, having a good cry actually does make someone feel better, something we seem to know intuitively as children. Tears relieve stress by removing some of the chemicals built up in the body from stress.[8] The opposite is also true: suppressing tears increases stress levels and contributes to diseases aggravated by stress, such as high blood pressure, heart problems, and peptic ulcers.[9] One study found that crying is more effective than any antidepressant on the market.[10] The old Jewish proverb, "What soap is for the body, tears are for the soul," supports the mounting scientific evidence.

Crying also helps us cope psychologically. It forces us to confront the situation. Naming what our tears are saying focuses the problem and points us in the direction of the solution. Some people fear that once they or a loved one start crying, they will never stop. However, in our personal and clinical experience, we have found tears, which may feel out of control, actually decrease a feeling of helplessness by calming us down as we allow them space. Tears open the doorway to growth. As Psalm 126:5 says, "May those who sow in tears reap with shouts of joy."

Sadness is a plea for empathy and compassion. It highlights our healthy dependency and is nature's way to appeal for another's help. The baby cries because it wants to be picked up. The good news is that receiving care is a win-win situation. Both the receiver and the giver feel better from the exchange. Think of moments in your life when you were able to comfort someone else. What an amazing gift to know that your presence could make such a difference. Sadness also has the power to unite people, something we witness at most funerals. Petty squabbles are put aside when sadness reminds us of what really matters: connections.

For over three years, I (George) ran a weekly ongoing grief group for parents who lost their firefighter sons at the World Trade Center after 9/11. The group provided a chance for parents to talk about their sons and express their sadness. They were all in the pain together, and they appreciated feeling understood. There were lots of tears but also tons of comfort and compassion. For most members the group became the highlight of their week. This grief group provided a space for each parent to be real and connect with others who could embrace their pain and not run away. Unlike the larger culture that avoided their sadness, these parents leaned in. An amazing thing happened as the sadness was shared: it led to greater love.

The positive view of sadness is captured by the Buddhist perspective that difficult circumstances are *necessary* for us to become happy. A famous Buddhist teaching states: "When obstacles arise, the wise rejoice while the foolish retreat."[11] One of the greatest sufferers of hurt and sadness is Jesus, a "man of sorrows and acquainted with grief" (Isa. 53:3). His life was one of continued sorrows, from the manger to the cross. Yet Jesus didn't fall into hopelessness and depression. His sadness opened his heart to be closer to God and others. He used adversity to love more deeply. Jesus understood the benevolent nature of tears.

Sadness is one of our greatest vehicles for repair. It pushes for connection and draws hearts toward us. The saddest thing isn't the tears when you are feeling down but having no one to hold you while you cry. Honoring the purpose of sadness to foster connection allows us to embrace the tears and use them to reach out to others and not put all our energies into avoiding our pain.

Fear

Fear can paralyze us and crush our hopes. Fear causes a change in brain and organ function and ultimately a change in behavior, such as fighting back, running away, freezing, or trying to appease. Fear may occur in response to a specific stimulus in the present or to a future situation that is perceived as a threat to health, status, power, security, or anything held valuable.[12]

Fear is the ultimate warning system, alerting us that there is danger. The signal happens rapidly, mobilizing us to act and reduce or avoid the threat. Scientists have discovered how easily fear, like our other emotions, can take charge and make decisions, bypassing the rational parts of our brain. If something jumps out of the shadows, we don't have time to think. Our bodies take over in an immediate flight response.

Like the rest of our emotions, fear is designed to be a temporary state. It quickly assesses a situation for risk and pushes for action. However, when fear is long lasting, it can ravage our health, taxing all of our body's systems and increasing the risk for a multitude of physical ailments. When temporary fears turn into a generalized, continual anticipation of negative consequences, then the body stays stuck in a perpetual fight-or-flight response. Visualize running a marathon every day with a lion chasing you. The toll of constant anxiety is enormous: anxiety disorders are the most common mental illness in the United States, affecting over forty million adults in the United States age eighteen and older (18 percent of the US population).[13] Even though many people in our society are affluent and enjoy frequent opportunities to unwind, we are being overwhelmed by fear. Our relentless pursuit of happiness combined with our constant attempts to escape fear are not working well.

The best way to deal with fear is to face it. Fear is not our enemy; it is our friend. Embedded in our fears are our hopes and dreams. Even chronic anxiety is trying to tell us something. Not listening to the signal prevents us from making the changes necessary to move forward. Buried fear still influences our behavior, but it often remains outside our awareness. We need to learn how to lean into fear and listen to its message.

Understanding the many benefits of fear can make it easier to embrace. Fear is a great motivator. Not only does it stay alert to a threat, but it also provides energy to respond. Fear keeps us going, rather than settling for complacency. Being afraid to let the team down allows members to push themselves past their limits. Fear of failure sparks creative energy and pushes us to stretch our limits. Often our greatest risks produce our greatest successes. Fear helps us focus and adjust to the demands of our environment. It tells us when to push and when to pull back.

Fear causes us to worry, and in the short term our brains like to worry because it provides a sense of control and ability to change our fate. Anxiety sharpens our focus and boosts our concentration.[14] For example, anxiety helps air traffic controllers stay alert. Air traffic controllers who are too happy make more mistakes than their more focused, anxious counterparts.

Realistic fears also assist us in saying no, setting limits, stopping risky behaviors, and appreciating the need for discipline. Fear of making mistakes makes us more efficient and effective. In our work with families, we see the fallout when children who don't learn the value of *no* become lazy, selfish, disrespectful, and out of control. Fear of disappointing parents and others can channel our energies in socially appropriate ways. Healthy fear can provide necessary guardrails in life.

We believe fear's greatest asset is the vulnerability it creates. Fear creates an opportunity for us to signal to others that we need help. Like sadness, it is a beacon calling for connection. Imagine a child awakening from a bad dream and calling out for help. A parent's gentle comfort bonds the two together. As strange as it may sound, take away the nightmare, and they lose the opportunity for connection.

Vulnerability entails risk because the outcome is uncertain. Vulnerability can lead to either rejection or closeness. Yet even in a worst-case scenario—taking a risk and being utterly rejected—that fear and pain also provides an opportunity for us to turn toward others for comfort. If we are courageous enough to show ourselves fully, exposing our fears and failings to those we love, then we give ourselves a chance to be truly seen and accepted unconditionally. One of the most fulfilling experiences in life is to be known in the fullness of our authenticity, not only in the places where we shine, but in the darkness where we hide.

I (George) will never forget playing in a baseball championship game when I was nine years old. The big hitter on the other team hit a monster fly ball to the outfield. I was playing right field, and I ran backward to catch the ball. Unfortunately, the ball bounced off my glove, striking me in the head and momentarily knocking me out. When I came to, my dad was holding an ice pack on my head. We lost the game, and I was scared my dad was disappointed with me. I'll never forget him taking me out to dinner afterward to celebrate me being such a good son and having such a hard head. To this day, I still carry his message that I'm loved unconditionally, even with my blunders.

When we feel isolated, fear can be terrifying. However, the darkness is not so scary when it is shared. The choice is crucial: we can use fear as a catalyst to turn toward others or use our energy to avoid and hide from fear until it eventually sneaks up and catches us. In 1 Peter 5:7 we are encouraged to cast all our anxieties on to God because God cares for us. We believe God uses fear as an instrument for connection. Fear leads us to God. When the Scriptures say, "Do not be afraid," we trust God is revealing his simple plan for turning fear into vulnerability, an opportunity to deepen relationship.

Shame and Guilt

The last of the so-called negative emotions are shame and guilt. Just thinking about shame and guilt can elicit bad feelings about ourselves and make us want to look away from others. Shame and guilt exist in every culture and are understood by every major religious tradition. Today, people often use the words *shame* and *guilt* interchangeably. However, there are important differences. Shame is a more global and painful feeling that something is bad or wrong with us personally. Guilt is a feeling of remorse caused by specifically doing something wrong. Simply put, guilt says, "I have done bad," while shame says, "I am bad." Both emotions can make us feel diminished and damage our self-esteem. Yet, shame is often more powerful and profound than guilt. Both emotions elicit feelings of being sorry, yet guilt tends to push us to make amends, while shame propels us to hide.

In the Hebrew Scriptures, Adam and Eve in the book of Genesis provide us with examples of what guilt and shame look like. Adam and Eve committed the first sin by biting into the alluring but forbidden fruit. This willful disobedience generated the first rupture in the relationship between God and humanity. We tend to focus on the initial act, biting the apple; however, the hiding that came afterward was even more crippling, and it speaks to the emotional consequences of the disobedience. Instead of going toward God with their sense of guilt to repair the relationship, Adam and Eve chose to cover their shame. They deliberately moved away from God and selected separation over connection. Being cut off from the connection of love is a fitting description of hell. Separation is the heart of all sin. At the very moment when we most need the support of others, we move away from them, which reinforces our isolation. We are left lonely and hidden.

A major drawback to this propensity to hide is that no one sees or understands what is going on inside of the person hiding. I (George) became aware of this when interacting with my son in a recent conversation. I had just read an article about how the brains of kids today are not developing the ability to read facial expressions because of not enough practice interacting with people. The core issue seems to be that they spend too much time watching electronic screens. As a therapist who knows the importance of reading emotions on faces, this scared the hell out of me. So I decided to read the article to my son CJ, who spends too much time playing video games. He sat down next to me as I carefully read him the article, emphasizing important passages. When I finished, he got up and said, "Dad, you know every time you read me something and try to help me, I feel bad about myself."

Wow! My attempt to love my son was training him to go away from me. Thank God he said something, and I was given a chance to change my ways and repair our relationship. But how many people just go away with diminished spirits and never express their pain? If CJ had hidden his pain and placated me with some head nodding, he would have been alone with his hurt. The intention of the person sending the message is not what matters; rather, how the message lands for the receiver is critical. CJ felt bad about himself after our interaction. He doubted my belief in him and his faith in himself.

It is my job as a parent to protect my son, even if that means delivering hard messages. But despite my noble intentions, if my interactions continually send signals to my son that he is doing something wrong, then I am chipping away at his essence and increasing the distance in our relationship. Criticism is like little punches to the brain, literally triggering the pain receptors in our heads. The more I criticize, sending CJ into shame, the easier it is the next time for both of us to enter that same critical-shaming cycle, strengthening these negative pathways. Creating new positive pathways is essential to closeness. To repair my relationship with CJ, I decided to cut down on my blaming, and the next evening, I read him a comedy with plenty of jokes in it to give his body an upbeat experience of reading with Dad.

What is so vicious about shame is that not only are we tortured by being cut off from connection, but also in our confinement, we turn on ourselves. When we are the most down and in need of help, we are utterly alone and treat ourselves with contempt. When we don't like ourselves, it is hard to believe we are lovable. Imagine being stuck in a scary dark hole and hating yourself for being so stupid for falling into the hole. Is there a worse abyss than thinking everyone dislikes you and hating yourself? Research is resoundingly consistent in its finding that the more shame a person feels, the more anxious, aggressive, and detached he becomes.[15] Shame thrives as a secret and becomes a tomb of our own making. In the long term, the more we try to outrun our shame, the more the isolation and pain grows.

One of my stories of shame occurred when I (Heather) was in sixth grade. I was the target of a bully's taunts and told I could not sit at the "cool" table in the classroom and needed to leave my seat. I got elbowed, and someone kicked me under the table. Later, I found cruel anonymous notes in my desk. The situation escalated, until the bully put Scotch tape in my hair, which the teacher had to cut out. It was then that I decided to concede and moved to the other girls' table. The bullying wasn't worth trying to be "cool"—or to make a point. Sometimes, we need to remove ourselves from the abuse. Even in recalling that story, I feel a sense of embarrassment and a fear that it could make you, my readers, think, "There must be something wrong with her. She must be flawed or defective." After many years of working to redeem stories of my past, I know that is not true. But the reality is that there is still a pocket of shame that I touch when retelling and reliving this story. As a result of this difficult experience, I was wary of getting too close to potential friends and imagined the script would repeat itself. With time, faith, and healing relationships, I was able to restore a sense of self-worth. Looking back, I see how that sixth-grade story helped deepen in me the capacity for empathy and compassion. I understood what it meant to be hurt and made a commitment to be a person who helps those who hurt.

The key to healing shame is bringing light into the darkness. When we can courageously confront the darkness instead of turning away, we are on the road to recovery. Brené Brown says the antidote to shame is empathy, from both ourselves and others.[16] By searching out and embracing our shadow side, we give ourselves a chance to shrink the darkness. When others come alongside our brokenness and cradle us with grace and compassion, our wounds heal. Self-compassion and loving responses from others are the key ingredients to transform shame into deeper security through connection.

For many people, the healing response that undoes the power of shame comes from a loving parent, a true love, or a sense of the Holy. Mystical theologians of different faith practices often describe a mystical union between one's soul and the divine spark—the Source or God. This deep knowing is a space of connection where we are filled with joy and experience an overpowering, all-encompassing love. One can imagine how a spiritual encounter of that magnitude could diminish one's sense of isolation and the need to hide. This mystical union offers the template to healing shame and for unconditional love and acceptance. We can offer that same message of love and worth to those around us as we reach toward them. We can be a part of the divine spark, illuminating others' darkness, helping them come to the light. It is one thing to be loved for all the good we do and our most flattering traits. It is another thing entirely to be loved in the midst of our failings, shortcomings, emotional outbursts, and small-mindedness.

Like all emotions, everything God creates serves a function, and to develop a more holistic perspective on shame, we need to appreciate its benefits. When we are feeling stuck and helpless, shame provides energy to move. If we can figure out what is wrong with us and fix it, then there is hope for a better outcome.

Shame offers us a sense of control, direction, and understanding and something for us to hold onto. Pinpointing the problem inside ourselves gives us hope for a different outcome if we can change who we are. Many of us just burrow deeper into the shame and hope doing so will motivate us to change. For example, shame might cause someone to look in the mirror with disgust and call herself a "fat pig" in a faulty attempt to motivate herself to lose weight. Her underlying belief is that identifying her character flaws of laziness and lack of discipline in controlling her eating might stimulate her to change her actions. Picture the abused little girl saying to herself "I'm a bad girl" and hoping that if she acted better, her life would improve. Sadly, our attempts to change ourselves to avoid bad things happening often fall far short of the intended goal.

The popular perception that shame is always bad blames people for developing these normal reactions to life's struggles. If shame didn't serve a purpose, however, it would not be so universal. Sometimes we actually do really bad things, and feeling bad can motivate us to improve our behavior. There are countless stories in sacred texts about how mistakes led to transformation. Like King David of the Hebrew Scriptures, sometimes our hubris and independence need to be broken by our failures so that we can turn back toward God and others and restore our relationships. Although shame often leaves us in dark places, it is not inherently evil. Feeling bad about ourselves signals disconnection and implores us to repair, to address the underlying need: connection.

Like all emotions, shame is informational. Avoiding the signal means avoiding the solution. Expanding the definition of shame empowers us to connect with and listen to the underlying needs. When we are mindful of our core needs for connection and the survival strategies we employ to protect ourselves, then we can decide the best way to get our needs met. If, instead of hiding, we actually used the energy of shame to turn toward connection, think how different our lives could be. What a different path to follow if Adam and Eve had actually run toward God and said, "We made a terrible mistake, and we need your help to understand what was wrong with us that propelled us to such a grievous act." Shame points us toward the opportunities for grace and for repairing what is wrong with the world and us. Its purpose isn't punishment but redemption. In Judaism, the faithful are called to *tikkun olam,* which means to repair or heal the world. All are called to play their part to restore and transform the brokenness of our world.[17] Overcoming shame by leaning into what it is telling us is part of healing our world and all those our lives touch.

The Beauty of Connection

Recognizing that all emotions provide neutral information that we can respond to negatively or positively, we now turn to the "positive" emotions of surprise and happiness. Surprise and happiness certainly signal good things happening, but they can also cast a dark shadow. Just as negative emotions hold the potential for good, the positive emotions carry the possibility for bad. Expanding the definition of all emotions to include both positive and negative elements ensures these tools have the greatest versatility and usefulness.

Surprise

At the heart of surprise is a state of "not knowing." Its main function is to immediately shift our attention to an unanticipated event. Our ordinary expectations and routine assumptions are interrupted by a fresh experience. Surprise is a great wake-up call that forces us to be radically aware of what is happening in the present. We have to notice something before we can act on it. Our cognitive thinking brain is too slow to comprehend and adapt to sudden changes in our environment.

Although surprise can be a response to both negative and positive events, we want to emphasize its impartial role as a messenger for change. Because stress and change are instrumental for growth, the amount of surprise in our lives is a good gauge of whether we are embracing or avoiding change. People who are risk takers and open to feedback discover surprises every day. Consistent, daily "not knowing" moments are physical markers that we are growing and continuing to learn. In contrast, those who need to feel in control work hard to make life predictable and eliminate surprises. They view change as a threat. Too many of us get stuck in our routines, choosing the comforts of predictability and control rather than the discomfort of stretching. Yet it is the ruptures and repairs that cultivate revitalization and expansion. Stress is an essential ingredient to flourishing. Surprise is confirmation that we are open to receiving feedback and engaging with our environment.

Depending on the triggering incident, surprise is often followed by other emotions. Someone menacingly jumping out of a dark alley or a scantily clad lover opening the door to welcome us for a dinner date both elicit a response of eyebrows rising and jaw dropping. Surprise immediately focuses attention and paves the way for other emotions to take over.

Surprise and Curiosity

We often interpret surprise as a positive emotion because of its frequent association with feelings such as excitement and curiosity. Surprise can propel us to try to understand. We all know the rush of energy when we are enthusiastically trying to figure something out. This yearning to explore seems to be in our God-given DNA. In the Hebrew Scriptures, the psalmist is curious and meditates on what God has created: "I remember the days of old, I think about all your deeds, I meditate on the works of your hands" (Ps. 143:5).

Maintaining a curious mind is essential to growth, both individually and as a species. Cultivating curiosity requires openness to the unfamiliar and courage to face possible failure. Humanity's greatest achievements are in large part a product of curiosity. Albert Einstein appreciated the value of surprise and curiosity. He said, "The important thing is not to stop questioning. I have no special talent. I am only passionately curious."[18] It is clear that we sometimes need to be curious and perhaps deviate from the norm if we hope to innovate. Surprise ensures we are awake and alive in the present moment.

As for its impact on relationships, increased curiosity is linked to stronger connections. It is easier to meet and maintain important relationships when we are open to others' points of view and interested in learning about them. Knowing your partner is interested in you is a huge component of building trust and security. Gallup polls from more than 130 nations report the two most common sources of happiness are engaging in good relationships and continuing to learn new things.[19] Both are natural outcomes of healthy curiosity.

Curiosity is good for your health, especially your brain. Studies suggest increased curiosity is associated with longer life, higher IQ scores, and a lower likelihood of developing hypertension, diabetes, and dementia.[20] Mental stimulation creates new neural pathways, which keep our brains growing. The more energy we invest in exploration and understanding, the more fully our passions blossom. The reverse is also true: declining curiosity is frequently associated with declining health.

However, sometimes curiosity hurts more than it helps. It certainly didn't help Adam and Eve. Think about how many explorers set off to discover new lands only to find misery, failure, and death. For many people, significant failures kill the desire to explore the unknown and lead them to choose safety over curiosity.

Appreciating both the upside and downside of curiosity is essential for developing appropriate flexibility. Too often we swing to one extreme side of the continuum, risking too much or too little. Some people put up walls and don't take risks to protect against bad things happening. However, walls that keep out bad also prevent the good stuff. Others recklessly throw caution to the wind, and their extreme pushing against the limits leads to their undoing.

The most important aspect of surprise and curiosity is the way they affect our relationships with ourselves, others, and God. As Martin Buber says, "All real living is meeting."[21] God seems to be inviting us all to join in the adventure. Encountering new experiences with an openness to be changed—like the journeys of Abraham, Jesus, Siddhartha Gautama (the Buddha), Muhammad, and Confucius—is at the heart of most world religions. These religions all encourage transformation, which surprises us and takes us out of our comfort zones but also gives us an expanded view of ourselves and our spiritual story. The Hebrew sacred texts read, "Surprise us with love at daybreak; then we'll skip and dance all the day long" (Ps. 90:14, Eugene Peterson's *The Message*). We are all invited to share in the hopefulness of surprise.

Happiness

It is fitting to end our discussion of emotions with happiness. We all want to be happy. Happiness is a state of well-being signified by positive emotions ranging from satisfaction to intense joy. We all are familiar with the warm sensations we feel when we are greeted with a big smile, hear a deep belly laugh, or receive a compassionate hug. Life at its best is a celebration. Often happiness is associated with love, because when our universal needs to be seen, accepted, understood, protected, comforted, and loved are met, then the result is the positive emotions, such as joy, hope, contentment, calmness, and peace.

Happiness plays an essential role in our survival, as it is a natural antidote to the harmful effects of stress and negative emotions. The "highs" of positive emotions keep us going, grinding away each day. Happiness is the reward for all the hard work. Happiness is so important to our existence that the founders of the United States built it into the Declaration of Independence, asserting that all people possess an inalienable right to life, liberty, and the pursuit of happiness. Barbara Fredrickson, a pioneering psychologist who researches positive emotions, believes happiness is humanity's evolutionary birthright. For thousands of years our ancestors passed down secrets and insights into living a happy life. These lessons are encoded in our DNA.[22] As a result, the universal nature of happiness transcends race, culture, and geography.

Happiness has astounding benefits. According to Fredrickson, not only does happiness counteract negative emotions, but it also helps build resources. Physically, happy people are more energetic, work out more frequently, and are overall in better health. They possess higher self-esteem, and because they feel good, it is much easier for them to put in the effort to maintain a healthy lifestyle. Conversely, eating right and exercising makes it easier to feel good, and a positive cycle is created. A whole slew of research is highlighting the benefits of happiness in increasing life expectancy, health, marital satisfaction, immune functioning, income, and job satisfaction.[23] Mentally, happiness increases our ability to learn and is associated with better grades. While negative emotions constrict the mind to focus on threats, happiness expands the mind to integrate new information. Happy people are more open. Curiosity thrives in optimism and shrinks in anxiety.[24] With all these benefits, given the choice, who wouldn't choose happiness?

Focusing too much effort on trying to be happy often makes it challenging to face discomfort and the negative emotions, however. Recent groundbreaking research supports the counterintuitive idea that striving for happiness may actually cause more harm than good. In fact, at times, the more people pursue happiness, the less happiness they seem able to obtain. Chasing happiness sets up high expectations and inevitable disappointment when the goals are not reached.[25] Trying to remain forever happy guarantees that when the inevitable disruptions occur, we experience them as a failure instead of an opportunity for growth. Overpursuing joy exiles the other emotions, sending them underground. A relentless pursuit of happiness actually set us up for depression.

In fact, as life gets easier—with all our comforts—our actual resiliency to handle adversity shrinks with too little practice. Many kids today feel entitled to a life of joy and relaxation, and yet this attitude is producing poor results.[26] Excessive ease and comfort equals a lack of stress and challenge. As we discussed earlier, too little stress means inertia and stagnation. It is hard to feel and deal with the darker emotions when we are spending so much energy trying to avoid them so we can be happy. A healthier understanding of happiness is that it comes and goes, that it is not meant to be a perpetual state.

We need an amalgamation of emotions to flexibly adjust to changing needs, not just a one-size-fits-all emotion. When we listen to the radio, the ability to shift between stations, not being stuck on your favorite station, provides the widest range of fulfilling entertainment. When we experience life's ups and downs, the ability to both tolerate negative emotions and engage in positive emotions is the ultimate sign of flexibility. Clearly, the more we appreciate the value of the downs in life, the greater our gratefulness for the highs. Knowing that happiness without other emotions is inadequate to fully experience the complexity of life, we can learn how to seize and truly appreciate joy when we are lucky enough to encounter it.

A balanced pursuit of happiness and joy, allowing for the full range of other emotions along the way, is the ideal environment to access our "true self" and best qualities. We can dream of future possibilities; we can focus on and feel compassion for others; we can experience a sense of peace and harmony within ourselves, our world and with our Creator. When we are happy, we have what we need. We are fully satisfied in the moment. What might our lives be like if we lived into the words of the important adage, "I have enough, I do enough, I am enough"? We could give up striving for more, better, bigger. We could accept who we are, good, bad, and ugly, and therefore be more tolerant of those traits in others. We would have the patience to wait for outcomes, to listen for divine whispers, to adopt a broader perspective on what is important in life. We could find peace on earth.

Many people of different religions believe God is love. If this is true, then joy must be God's gift to us to express the beauty of connection. According to Richard Rohr, a Franciscan friar and inspirational speaker, we all began as an expression of God's desire for relationship. The universe is ever expanding, and God wants our full participation. We began in beauty and union, and our destination is beauty and union.[27] What an amazing, hopeful message. Despite all the crazy ups and downs of life, the start and end point are the same, union with love. Each day is an invitation to come home, to love, and to enjoy our birthright to be secure in eternal relationship.

Part 2

How Stress Breaks and Makes Relationships

After exploring how stress impacts us individually, it is time to think about how stress dramatically affects relationships. Stress is such a normal part of everyday life that most of us don't pay attention to its symptoms. If we are unaware of its influence in our own bodies, then it is highly unlikely we realize how our stress is touching the lives of those around us. Like an unknown virus, stress gets passed around. Ignoring it only spreads the infection.

In the chapters ahead, we will look at how the movement from distress to eustress, from pain to healing, plays out in different facets of our lives. We will continue to emphasize the two tools for shifting distress into eustress. Sometimes when we are in distress, we can simply step back and reframe whatever is challenging for us (see it a new way). However, when distress is not so easily reframed, we can process the emotions—move into, deal with, and work through the distress to get to what is positive on the other side. Part of the destructive power of distress is the fact that we often feel lonely and isolated due to the complexities of life bearing down on us. But when we become aware we are not alone and have others in the boat with us, then our perspective can shift and our ability to cope is expanded. In our personal and clinical experience, we have seen that when people can move toward others, even if that other is God, we are able to find meaning, healing, and transformation in that connection.

Stress can lead to deeper harmony in relationships or to immense suffering. Our choice is simple: unite or allow stress to turn us against each other. We also can face stress better when we have a trusted companion. A Vietnam veteran shared a helpful story with me (George) in a therapy session. He said that during the war, one night each month his platoon of a hundred soldiers was broken up into single units, and each soldier was responsible for guarding a certain section of a pipeline. The experience of guarding the pipeline alone was horrible. The soldiers dreaded the task, and many would get physically sick days before their tour even started. Thankfully, the officers listened to their complaints and adjusted their tactics. Instead of separating the soldiers, they broke them up into pairs and doubled their area of responsibility. Realistically, it made no difference in their ability to guard the pipeline. The enemy could sneak up and eliminate two soldiers as easily as one. Yet, it made all the difference to the soldiers. Having someone to lean on and face the fear with makes a huge difference. To get a sense of the powerful infectious nature of stress, let's turn our attention to the most basic of interpersonal units: romantic relationships.

We are using the term *romantic relationships* to describe two people in a committed relationship who share a sense of mutual respect and admiration. The majority of people on this planet choose to get married, so when we discuss romantic relationships, we are mostly focusing on married couples. Yet, we are less concerned with what you call the relationship than we are with emphasizing the reciprocal nature of all romantic relationships. Regardless of the title of the relationship, when two people in love are exposed to stress, their relationship can turn into a sanctuary or a battlefield.

The miraculous thing about stress is that it can nudge us into vulnerability if we let it, which can transform our life and every relationship we have. Vulnerability is the doorway that allows us to meet God in the present moment. Vulnerability is courageously taking off your mask and showing the real you hiding inside. Vulnerability is the opposite of avoidance; it is authentically embracing our real feelings. Authenticity, not achievement, needs to be our main pursuit. Letting down our walls is the only way we give our true self a chance at responsiveness and comfort.

Chapter 4 provides an overview of stress's impact on romantic relationships, including the sexual dimension of relationships. Chapter 5 focuses on parenting issues within relationships.

We encourage you to also download our resource "Redeeming Loss and Stress," which deals with a variety of relationship losses, including those resulting from affairs, addictions, aging, and dying. You can find a link to this resource on the SkyLight Paths webpage for *Sacred Stress.*[28]

Now, we turn to the many ways stress can break or make relationships.

CHAPTER 4

Nurturing the Ultimate Connection

Romantic Relationships, Sex, and Stress

Is stress in a relationship good or bad? Stress brings out the best and worst in all of us. The key factor is how the stress is handled. There is no denying that pain is inflicted on everyone when distress destroys safety in homes. However, stress is vital and necessary in relationships. We hope that by this point in *Sacred Stress*, when you hear the word *stress* you recognize the positive nature of stress and also realize you can transform distress into growth. The combination of both thinking differently and actually working through stress in new ways sets up flourishing relationships. We'll look at the challenges stress can present to relationships, and then we'll talk about how those challenges can transform us.

Negative Impact of Stress on Relationships

Stress is intensified in a relationship because stress is contagious, affecting not just an individual's stress levels (and health) but also his partner's.[1] No wonder a bad day at work often turns into a fight at home. Our partners have a choice, though. They can become part of the problem (our distressed state) or the solution, by helping us calm down and reconnect.

In a fascinating experiment to test the transmissible nature of emotions, researchers asked three audiences to listen to and rate a speech delivered by an actor. Each actor delivered the same speech but in different emotional tones. The first actor's tone was upbeat and positive. The second actor's speech was neutral and unremarkable. The last actor's manner was negative and depressed. Not surprisingly, the positive tone scored best with the audience, while the negative speech scored lowest. Even more interesting was how the audience members felt about themselves. After listening to each speech, the audiences members described feeling in a state similar to the tone in which the speech was delivered.[2] Mirror neurons in our brains hardwire us to feel what others around us are feeling. Spend ten minutes around someone who spreads joy, and you start feeling elated.

Given this natural propensity to share emotional states, it makes sense that bad relationships are harmful to our well-being. John Gottman, a pioneer in studying marriages, can predict divorce in couples with over 90 percent accuracy. His research into "master couples" and "disaster couples" shows that disaster couples handle stress poorly by turning against each other and are characterized by criticism, defensiveness, contempt, and stonewalling.[3] These four factors are ways of protecting the individual at the cost of the partner. All couples experience some of these traits, but when they become chronic, it spells the almost certain demise of the relationship.

Master couples, on the other hand, develop the crucial ability to turn toward each other. They fight over the same issues as disaster couples. Yet, they are able to maintain trust, kindness, and closeness. In these strong marriages, partners understand that stress provides an opportunity for growth and greater love. Depending on the state of the relationship, the same stressful event affects different couples in very different ways.

Master couples are able to sustain the magic ratio of five positive interactions for every negative interaction.[4] So if you are keeping score at home and you find yourself lucky enough to be in a relationship where compliments are offered five times as often as criticism, then you are in the rare master couple category. When we as therapists discovered this magic ratio, we started to use it as the basis for homework assignments. Encouraging couples to pay attention to this ratio and keep a running tally seemed like a simple way to ensure a good connection. Unfortunately, it turns out it is really hard to compliment and not criticize when you are feeling distant from your partner. Despite a good intention, a positive comment sounds artificial and inauthentic in an atmosphere of mistrust and tension. Simply saying complimentary words doesn't create a positive interaction. Positive feelings must be present first. Positivity is the natural by-product of connection, and master couples have the ability to repair any offense or breach of trust that has occurred in order to maintain closeness.

Interestingly, the ratio for disaster couples is 0.08 compliments for every 1 criticism, so there is a lot less of the good stuff to counterbalance all the negativity.[5] No wonder the bank of goodwill runs dry so quickly. Master and disaster couples live in two totally different worlds.

Looking at how our brains work provides insight into how the quality of the connection between partners dramatically affects the way we experience stress. It appears our nervous systems are created to be captured by other nervous systems. Susan Johnson, the founder of Emotionally Focused Therapy, and James Coan, a neuroscientist studying brain activity, conducted a study of married women's brains using fMRI scans to see in real time what was happening when they faced threat.[6] While in the fMRI machine, the women were told a flashing letter X meant they had a 20 percent chance of receiving a shock on their ankles. But in different iterations of the experiment, the brain responded in startlingly different ways.

When alone in the machine, the letter X triggered the women's brains to light up like a Christmas tree, and they described the shock as intense. For women in distressed marriages and whose partners were holding their hands in the experiment, the X again lit up the brain and the pain was labeled as severe, even worse than being alone. (Science supports the old adage that being in a bad marriage feels lonelier than being alone.) Interestingly, when a stranger held the women's hands, the X triggered moderate brain activity, and the shock was described as moderate. When women fortunate enough to be in strong, healthy marriages held the hands of their husbands, their brains hardly reacted at all, and the pain was regarded as mild to nonexistent.

It is important to note that the pain level administered in every test was exactly the same. How the brain reacts to stress, threat, and pain correlates to the degree of closeness in the relational bond. If our brain perceives our partner as a source of safety, then stress is not so scary and pain is easier to manage. Unfortunately, the opposite is also true. If our partner is a seen as a threat, then that same stress becomes a huge burden.

If I (George) want to go to the Yankees game with a few friends and my wife, Kathy, and I are in a good place, then it is no big deal. If we are in a bad place, it is a huge deal. My going out with friends confirms Kathy's feeling of rejection and my inability to notice the distance. It is not about the Yankees game; it's about the state of our relationship in that moment. If you were looking at my brain under an fMRI machine when my wife asks me, "How is your day going?" you would see that different parts of my brain get triggered, depending on where we are as a couple. When our connection is strong, my prefrontal cortex, the region of the brain tasked with cognitive functioning, assumes Kathy's intent is good, and I respond positively: "Thanks for asking. It's great. How's your day?" However, if Kathy and I are in a more distressed place, then that same question triggers a different part of my brain to engage, the amygdala, which is responsible for emotional reactivity. The amygdala is like a vigilant soldier guarding against attack.[7] With my amygdala taking charge, my response is very different: "What do you think I did all day but bust my hump? Did you do anything productive today?" The same question leads to very different outcomes, depending on where the relationship stands. Negativity breeds further negativity. Figuring out how to get the right parts of our brains to respond is a worthwhile investment of time and energy.

So Why Do People Get Married?

Given the immense challenges of marriage, we have to wonder why people get married in the first place. I (George) grew up in a big family in a tough blue-collar town, and I was surrounded by struggling families. Dysfunction and unhappiness characterized most of the marriages I witnessed. I remember thinking at an early age that I was never going to get married. At twenty-two years old I joined the NYPD and served three years as a NYC police officer, which only strengthened my resolve to not join the misery club. I responded to countless domestic dispute calls and vowed to never make the same mistake as all these miserable couples. It was crystal clear to me that the partners' failure to communicate was exacerbating their distress and reducing the quality of their lives. In these shaky relationships, not only did they do little to support each other, but they actually assisted in bringing each other down. I later joined the NYC fire department and again found myself surrounded by hundreds of complaints about the ills of marriage. I recall pondering to myself, *What are people looking for in marriage?* Whatever it was they were searching for, I was confident I didn't need it.

But soon enough, I met Kathy, and the world quickly turned upside down. High on the neurochemicals of oxytocin and dopamine, I fell in love, and like everyone else, I believed my marriage would prove the exception. Finding someone special, who shared my brain, finished my sentences, and liked my quirks made the relationship worth investing time and energy in. Our ability to share our thoughts and emotions was amazing. I never experienced such unconditional love and acceptance. Together, we became part of something bigger and better than our separate selves. Discovering our mutual devotion and responsiveness to each other liberated our hidden dreams for deeper intimacy. Realizing the universal truth, that if I "do not have love, I am nothing" (1 Cor. 13:2), I jumped off the cliff and committed my heart to another.

Why did I do it, in spite of the many disaster marriages I had witnessed? It seems human beings have an innate desire to experience deeper intimacy in a dynamic relationship with another. This universal longing for connection is captured well in a phrase in Ephesians 5:31: "the two will become one flesh." Religions emphasize our divine calling to be in relationship. Most people believe we are created for the give and take of relationships and are incomplete alone.

Interestingly enough, science is saying the same thing. Scientist Matthew Lieberman in his book *Social: Why Our Brains Are Wired to Connect* stresses the evolutionary importance of social bonds.[8] Across multiple studies examining creatures from the smallest rodents all the way to us humans, the data strongly implies connection is as important to our survival as food, water, and shelter. As one research observes, "Being socially connected is our brain's lifelong passion because it's been baked into our operating system for tens of millions of years."[9]

Psychologist Kelly McGonigal believes "stress makes us social," and she explains what happens in our body when we experience stress.[10] During a stress response, the body releases many hormones, all mobilizing the body to fight or flight. However, most people are unaware that oxytocin, sometimes called the "cuddle hormone," is also released during the stress response. Oxytocin serves two primary functions. First, it is a natural anti-inflammatory that helps us stay relaxed during stress. Second and most importantly, oxytocin primes us to reach out to friends and family for support. McGonigal says, "Our stress response is nudging us to tell someone how you feel instead of bottling it up. When life is difficult, your stress response wants you to be surrounded by people who care about you."[11] Clearly, if our bodies are created to release oxytocin during stressful situations, then connection is important to our Maker. It's unnatural to face threat alone. No wonder Jesus's distress was so intense when he felt cut off from his Father during the passion. "My God, My God, why have you forsaken me," he called out (Matt. 27:46 NLT).

When religious scholars and scientists agree, you know their common ground is fairly indisputable. The consensus is declaring our universal need for others in order to feel whole and complete.

If we are created and wired for connection, then getting married, despite its challenges, is a plausible enterprise. Regardless of the drawbacks, the positive statistics about marriages are quite impressive. Married people live longer, make more money, are better educated, are healthier, and enjoy more stable families.[12] When we (George and Heather) were each single, these statistics seemed confusing. If most marriages are failing and overwhelmed with stress, then it seems logical that single people should be the symbols of optimal health. Imagine the hassle-free existence of living in a bachelor pad doing whatever you wanted, whenever you pleased. Sounds too good to be true. Well, it is. Multiple studies indicate that even people in bad marriages enjoy statistical benefits that bachelors do not.[13] Despite marital stress and discord, being in relationship means partners at least get moments of connection when their nervous systems can relax. Bachelors may avoid a lot of the pitfalls, but they also miss out on the good stuff of relationships. Avoidance correlates with less connection and poorer health. We all share a basic human need for a response— to be seen, to matter, to be loved. None of us can escape the existential question, "If I am in need, will someone be there?" Answering this question with a maybe is better than no. When the answer is an unequivocal yes, anything is possible.

Why Is Marriage So Difficult?

If all the evidence points in the same direction, underscoring our fundamental necessity for intimate relationships, then why is maintaining healthy marriages so difficult? Our culture romanticizes marriage and makes it look easy. We think true love shouldn't require hard work, just the right chemistry. As we point out repeatedly in this book, however, our working definitions really matter. Seeing marriage as an achievable fairy tale sets us up for high expectations and, ultimately, failure. Yes, we can live happily ever after, but we need to learn how to navigate the ups and downs. Inevitable distress strikes all relationships, and if couples don't learn how to rally together, then their disappointment may turn into frustration and criticism of their partner.

We believe American pastor Timothy Keller's definition of marriage is much healthier: a holy union where two flawed people join together for mutual fulfillment through mutual sacrifice.[14] Marriage is a combination of hard work and grace. The goal in marriage isn't unconditional love and acceptance but to truthfully and lovingly hold up a mirror so each partner can grow. Each spouse's primary job is to help the other become his or her best self. A realistic view of marriage as both fun and hard work honors its purpose and creates healthy expectations. This reframed thinking allows couples to see the opportunity in distress to unite together.

Many of us don't get the help we need to develop a healthy perspective and learn the skills necessary to work through distress in relationships. We find ourselves simultaneously pulled to be in connection and to protect ourselves when our needs are not being met. No wonder intimate relationships can feel so crazy making. Understanding the predictable ways we miss each other in relationships can improve our ability to repair and create more rewarding connections.

For those of us courageous enough to risk joining with another, there are no guarantees. In order to receive, we need to risk asking; in order to give, we need to risk engaging. Either asking or giving is a gamble when we are unsure whether or how our partner will respond. Picture a little girl falling in her dance recital and looking out into the audience only to find her parents' critical eyes. Because her parents don't allow her to be sad, her unmet need for compassion and comfort gets buried deep inside.

When stress threatens relationships, we tend to either withdraw (pull away) or pursue (go on the offensive). In withdrawal we attempt to avoid the possible pain of rejection and failure by not risking engagement. Yet not risking ensures our defenses cut us off from a fulfillment that can only be found in relationships. In pursuit we protest and try to push our partner into responding, only to desperately notice it often doesn't work. Both strategies tend to result in isolation rather than connection.[15] But if we take a closer look at both of these strategies, we can understand how they can help us to handle distress.

Don't be concerned with trying to identify as either the withdrawer or the pursuer. In most relationships, partners fluidly change defensive positions. For example, the majority of time in my (George's) marriage, I withdraw. Yet when it comes to initiating sexual intimacy, I tend to take on the role of pursuer. I am critical when my wife is not in the mood, and she tends to pull away. What is important is to realize how one partner's behavior triggers a response in the other, and the other's reply then prompts further reactivity in the partner. In a matter of seconds, partners are caught in a mutually constructed feedback loop. Recognizing the interdependency of behaviors empowers couples to work together to change their moves. This is the antidote to pointing the finger at each other and hoping the other is fixed.

Understanding the World of Withdrawers

Why do people withdraw and emotionally disengage? Whenever we ask this question at trainings all over the world, the answer we receive is unanimous: we withdraw to protect ourselves. While this is true, withdrawal also has positive functions. For many withdrawers, turning off their emotions and focusing on cognitive tasks is a way to feel good about themselves.

Imagine firefighters running into a burning building. Their ability to turn off their fears and take care of their responsibilities is essential for the team's success. A firefighter certainly doesn't want to hear from the firefighter crawling next to her that the teammate is feeling scared and vulnerable. Expressing "sensitive feelings" in the heat of battle does not help the team do its job. Crawling through a room on fire to search for possible victims beyond the fire takes intense focus and courage. This ability to emotionally detach and turn off fear allows for heroic acts. When a whole apartment is engulfed in fire, some firefighters can crawl through five rooms of fire. Afterward, the firefighter who can go "five rooms deep" is shown great respect and becomes the one to emulate. Turning off emotions isn't just a defensive strategy; at times, it is a commendable and life-saving choice.

Appreciating the healthy functions of withdrawal makes it easier for nonwithdrawers to understand and come alongside them and connect, rather than accuse them of doing something wrong. Our society honors the ability to perform well under pressure and emotionally disengage. Do you want your doctor about to perform surgery sharing his doubts and insecurities? The Wall Street executive who calmly closes a pressured deal is showered with affirmation. Withdrawing and turning down their emotions is often what they do to feel best about themselves, to stay in control and focused.

Withdrawal that is flexible and adaptive is very beneficial. However, withdrawal that becomes habitual in all settings is disastrous to relationships. Often behavior that ensures success at work comes at a huge price at home. The armor used to hide feelings while carrying out professional missions is difficult to remove when off duty. Withdrawers believe the best way to protect themselves, and their relationship, during stressful times is to pull away to diffuse the situation. Waiting for the storm to pass becomes the go-to strategy.

In spite of this default of moving away, withdrawers do have a desire and longing to be close and connected to their partners. Unfortunately, the path to get there can be difficult and challenging. Withdrawers often say their experience of trying to connect is like walking across a minefield. As a withdrawer attempts to respond and connect, each step is fraught with anxiety and pressure. At any moment, he anticipates a sudden fight or criticism; oftentimes his partner's emotions feel like a mine blowing up. He wants to be connected and safe on the other side with his partner, but the path to get there is treacherous.

As the withdrawer continues to walk across the minefield, ever hopeful of connection, he develops an external focus, constantly scanning the environment for threats. All of his attention is focused on outside hazards. He is trying to respond properly, trying to stay in tune with his partner, and there is little room left for what is happening on the inside. Withdrawers concentrate on their performance to stay alive and not their own feelings. Walking through a minefield, each successful step brings some relief but also the inevitable nervousness about the next step. All energy is directed to the task at hand, getting through the minefield. Focus on the other side becomes difficult, and so the withdrawer frequently chooses to step off the field.

From the outside, it looks like nothing is going on or the withdrawer doesn't really care, when actually there is a lot going on inside a withdrawer, which no one sees.

Imagine this: you are standing on the edge of a minefield, and you are trying to get to the other side. You take a step, and everything is OK. And yet, you are uncertain of your next step because you know there is a mine somewhere. You take another step anyway because you really want to get to the other side to your loved ones. Your focus and anticipation are intense as your foot touches the ground. Whew, another step closer! You plant your foot firmly on the ground. Can you afford to pause and celebrate this momentary release of tension? No, you can't, when you know you have more steps to take. You take another step; your foot touches the ground. Boom! You just blew up. The worst part for withdrawers isn't even when things blow up. It's not knowing when the bomb is going to go off that is so insidious and makes surveying the landscape a 24/7 job. Relationships for withdrawers are loaded with threat and possible detonation. If you could retreat and avoid walking the minefield, wouldn't you do it? Withdrawers find respite from the pressures of relationships (minefield) by escaping into nonthreatening environments. Television, a sporting event or a beer, all offer pressure relief.

As long as withdrawers can get it right, they are safe. They love to fix problems, because solutions are the best way to reduce danger. Performance equals lovability. Unfortunately, it's impossible to always get it right. Hearing the message they are doing it wrong triggers a threat to the relationship. Withdrawers have learned to pull away into their own worlds to avoid conflict. However, the tragedy is that in isolation, no one sees their struggle.

Picture a little boy feeling scared when his parents are fighting. Both parents are so caught up in their own reactions they don't see their son struggling. Over time, this boy learns to depend on himself, because others are not going to show up for him in his time of need. His best options are to work hard to avoid contributing to his parents fighting and to go away to ride out the storm when they are fighting. No one helps him put words to his vulnerable feelings, so they become vague and unspoken. When he gets older, he finds a job that rewards this ability to turn off feelings. His inclination to be self-reliant is reinforced and admired.

Eventually, this young man marries and hears from his wife in a fight there is something wrong with him because he doesn't emotionally engage. Years of distancing himself from his feelings have ensured a large gap in his ability to understand his own interior world. He tries to protect himself and the relationship by going away to reduce the danger. He is just following the rules that worked in the past, and yet the message he receives is that the distance is his fault.

The good news is if we identify the problem, it also reveals the answer.

If your partner is withdrawing: If you can work to understand the withdrawer's world, he can begin to enjoy the benefits of openness and exploration. We all learn how to engage and give empathy by receiving it first. Withdrawers are blamed for what they didn't receive; give them a taste of empathy, and it is natural for them to give it back. By giving your partner the gift of permission for wanting to escape the pressures of failure, you can help your withdrawer engage and experience the value of connection. Acknowledge his fears and the helplessness of not knowing what to do and offer your compassion. This isn't just healing for the withdrawer, it is incredibly empowering for *you*. You get to be the special and powerful person who provides unconditional love.

If you are withdrawing: If you can shift your focus from your external performance to your own vulnerabilities, you can begin to notice your internal signals, which are telling you what you need. Practicing the four steps of embracing your emotions will empower you to know yourself and begin the healing process of getting the comfort you deserve.

If you have learned to pull away for good reasons, then you need to be able to discover the value of coming forward. It is life changing for someone used to being valued only for performing to actually experience love in failure. When you are accepted in your broken places, then you can trust the love given. It is counterintuitive, but risking letting your partner into your fears of failing creates new responses and actions in the relationship. In this atmosphere of reciprocal tenderness, we often witness withdrawers shift from feelings of pressure, anxiety, and exhaustion to being energized, relaxed, calm, curious, decisive, and confident.

Following the blueprint laid out earlier, we can see that the new insight (reframing) and the new strategy (embracing emotions) allow us to effectively relate to one another differently. A new understanding sets the stage to risk new moves. The withdrawer who experiences the benefits of connection after a fight or failure becomes less reluctant to engage. The numbed protection of withdrawal pales in comparison to the vibrancy of connection.

Understanding the World of Pursuers

When pursuers encounter walls in others and are left on the outside, they bang loudly for connection. Like a little child, they settle for negative attention rather than nothing at all. Fighting is a better option than isolation because there is still hope for connection in a fight. As with withdrawers, to truly understand pursuers we must honor the function of their anxiety and not just highlight its shortcomings. When isolation is the worst-case scenario, then generating a response is imperative for survival. Because of their determination to connect, pursuers tend to be more attuned to relationship needs in general. They usually are more comfortable with dependency and accessing their needs. They are more practiced at thinking about relationships and communicating their needs. Pursuers are also sensitive to connection problems and are quick to jump in and attempt to repair them.

Bids for attention, engagement, and feedback can be positive or negative and taken as plea or protest. For pursuers, there is nothing like a good scream to get people to listen. Pursuers regularly are the ones who reach toward the partner for connection, although their partners often interpret this as blame. When you understand that fighting is a better option than isolation, then it is easier to see why pursuers sometimes use anger and criticism to get a response. They hate their hyperreactivity, but the fear of nothing happening if they don't push is a strong motivator. Being angry with their partner temporarily keeps away the pain of rejection. Ironically, the criticism shows their hope that something can change.

To really appreciate the pushing, we need to understand how pursuers experience the absence of connection. Silence feels like deep rejection and breaks the interpersonal bridge that keeps partners together.[16] The pain of aloneness is unbearable for pursuers. Often the more they are disconnected from the relationship, the worse they feel about themselves. A partner may see criticism directed at him, but internally the pursuer often worries there is something wrong with him. How else do you make sense of constantly not being chosen? Go back in time to kindergarten. Who do we blame when no one picks us to be on the team? Ourselves. Every round of pursuit and rejection reinforces shame and increases anxiety.

Unfortunately, the pursuer's tendency to constantly protest leads the withdrawer to pull away further. As the withdrawer continues to disengage, the pursuer feels fear and frustration, becoming more consumed with the hurt of being rejected and losing the flexibility to see how hostile actions only increase the partner's need for protection. As the stress builds, each partner's range of behaviors shrinks.

If your partner is pursuing: Recognize her anger is born out of her desperation to connect, not an indictment of your performance. Visualize going to a shameful place inside yourself where you feel small and unlovable. Now stay in this ugly place where you hate yourself and doubt anyone cares. If that is not hard enough, now imagine sharing this vulnerable experience with your partner, who has a history of disappearing, and picture yourself hoping that this time, he is going to respond.

To get an additional sense of how challenging it is for your partner to risk vulnerability, imagine playing the game of falling backward and having your partner catch you. Your partner promises to catch you, so you close your eyes and reluctantly let yourself fall backward. As you expectantly wait for reassuring hands, you suddenly realize something is wrong and—whack! You hit the ground hard. Your partner apologizes for being distracted and asks you to try again. It is certainly hard to trust, but you long to feel connected, so you try again. Bam! It hurts even more the second time you crash. How angry are you and how stupid do you feel? Will you try again? It certainly is hard to risk when there is a track record of hurt and disappointment. The pursuer vacillates anxiously between seeking connection and fearing rejection.

What is so unfair for pursuers is they learn to mistrust only because others let them down. They protest the hurt of being let down and fight for better results. Then they are blamed because they are "too much"—for example, too needy, too emotional—and they begin to believe it. What can be worse than living in distress when no one wants to listen to your anguish? To liberate your partner from this anxiety trap, you need to love her in her broken places. Asking for this love is the ultimate risk, because showing vulnerabilities opens us up for rejection and the confirmation of our darkest fears. If you can lovingly respond in your partner's dark places, then the relationship will be cemented in security.

If you are pursuing: Like a withdrawer, a pursuer finds freedom in finding connection and compassion. Coming forward in a soft, vulnerable way, not leading with anger, is the pathway toward redemption. The possibility of being received lovingly by your partner can outweigh the risk of exposure.

What is so life-giving about this exchange is the healing impact for both partners; the pursuer receives comfort for his insecurities and the withdrawer is affirmed for her engagement. The pursuer's anxiety, anger, and criticism are replaced with peace, joy, contentment, and thankfulness. First recognizing and reframing the pursuit, then embracing the deeper feelings driving them both leads to connection and transformation.

Seeing the Negative Cycle in Action

Both protective strategies of withdrawing and pursuing result in more separation and defensiveness. As the hope of direct connection diminishes, the only routes left to get our needs met are circuitous and indirect. The more reactive the relationship becomes, the more each partner's ability to process his or her own individual vulnerability shrinks. Ignoring or not understanding our own emotional signals leaves both partners helplessly lost. Our defenses numb our ability to listen to the story that every emotion has to say. This defensive feedback loop continuously produces isolation and unmet needs, making life about avoiding potential hurt at the cost of long-term attachment.

To illustrate how these two protective strategies interact and create predictable patterns of behaviors, let's look at an exchange between me (George) and my wife, Kathy, that occurred a few years back. I was racing home from a tour at the firehouse, excited to join my family for dinner, spend some time with my kids, and maybe have a little alone time with my wife after the kids went to bed. As I opened the front door, Kathy shouted out, "Hey, did you get the milk?" Immediately, my stomach clenched. Guess what? I didn't get the milk. Typical of many men, being able to "get it right" is what makes me feel safe, important, and valued. So when I hear the message "I'm getting it wrong," I don't feel good, which is usually a prelude to a fight. I've learned over the years that talking about my feelings only tends to fuel a greater combustion. The best thing I can do to protect the relationship and myself is to go off by myself to calm down. I decided to go upstairs and check my emails.

My wife's version of the story is slightly different, as she remembers asking me nicely, "Honey, did you get a chance to pick up the milk?" The next thing she remembers is me walking past her and heading upstairs without a word. Immediately, she felt tightness in her chest and a feeling of rejection. After spending the day talking to little kids, she was looking forward to an adult conversation, and all of a sudden I didn't seem interested. Feeling hurt and alone, her body flooded with anxiety, mobilizing her to fix the problem. If the worst-case scenario is a rebuff, then fighting is a better outcome than separation. Despite her reactivity and tension, Kathy believed the only hope for repair was to talk. So Kathy predictably decided to follow me up the stairs and say, " I don't get it. I asked you one little favor. You can't even remember to do one simple thing."

My trigger to move into a defensive posture is the message that I'm failing, and that was precisely what Kathy was telling me. No wonder I didn't want to have a conversation. Feeling cornered, I protected myself by fighting back and saying, " I don't know why I came home. I should have stayed at work, where no one nags me." For many withdrawers, work is a safer place, because they get tons of affirmation and little criticism. My message perfectly reinforced Kathy's underlying fear of rejection. I was telling her I'd rather be at work than with her. You can see the negative cycle of protection picking up momentum.

Kathy, feeling hurt and misunderstood, pushed me to see the error of my ways. Maybe if she can give me proof of my failures, I can admit my mistakes and promise to change my ways. So Kathy tells me, "Sure, all you do is work. Your kids don't even know who you are." The scorecard is out, and she lets me know I'm coming up short in many areas. If I'm going to pick work over her, then she is going to point out the costs of my decision. Again, is there any wonder why I don't want to talk? Not only am I receiving the message that I'm failing on the little things, but now I'm also failing as a father. As my fears are confirmed, my urge for self-protection heightens. Hoping to create distance, I say, "Well, I have no choice. I wouldn't have to work so much if you didn't spend so much money." Clearly my tone is sending direct signals to Kathy that I'd prefer not to be around her. As each of us protects ourselves further, we fuel the need for greater fortification.

As Kathy's frustration mounts, so does her condemnation. She proceeds to tell me, "My mother was right about you. You're Mr. Undependable." Wow. Not only am I failing on so many levels, but now I hear her mother knew it all along! The neural pathways in my brain that want to avoid confrontation expand. As each wave of self-protection passes, it increases the likelihood of future brain signals reinforcing that strategy. I respond to Kathy by saying, "Funny, you should mention your mom, because my mom said, 'Be careful, because no woman will ever make you happy.'" With absolute precision I sent a signal to Kathy telling her she is too much and that, ultimately, she is destined to be left alone. In a matter of minutes we went from talking about the milk to each other's mothers. How did this happen so quickly?

When stress triggers self-protection, our default settings kick in without our awareness. In a flash, my energy is to withdraw, while Kathy's is to push. We use two very different energies to achieve the same, common goal: self-protection. We both learned these strategies before we met each other, and if we find ourselves in new relationships in the future, we will probably replicate similar patterns. If Kathy and I visit a marriage therapist for help and we focus on the surface topics, trying to resolve the many issues such as chores, kids, money, and extended families, progress is unlikely. Most couples are fighting about the same issues over and over again. John Gottman's research tells us 69 percent of the issues we fight about are perpetual and are never resolved throughout the relationship.[17] The point isn't to pay attention to issues but instead to focus on the emotional bond.

Chances are what you are fighting over today is still going to annoy you in twenty years. There is so much emphasis on fixing problems, and yet psychological research reveals advice is effective only 5 to 10 percent of the time.[18] The majority of issues cannot be fixed; it is the process of communication that matters. It is essential to shift the level of communication from the surface topics and tune into our emotional connection. Deep down we all want to trust that if we need our partner, he or she will be there for us. Logically, both Kathy and I believe we can depend on each other. However, when you look at our fight and understand our underlying vulnerabilities—my fear of failure and her fear of abandonment—we realize that, at times, we are not there for each other and actually are experts at perfectly reinforcing each other's fears.

If we can understand our cycle, we can recognize that our responses are not going to produce the results we hope for. Kathy's fear of rejection pushes her to talk in the hope that I will engage. My fear of rejection pushes me to pull away in the hope that Kathy can calm down. My withdrawal feeds Kathy's anxiety and fear of rejection; it doesn't calm her down. Her anxiety feeds my withdrawal and fear of failure; it doesn't reassure me. The key is for both of us to acknowledge that our need for self-protection is creating distance and mistrust. We need to reframe our thinking to unite us, rather than replay the negative pattern. What a gift it is for each partner to give permission to the desire for self-protection instead of blaming each other. Although Kathy's criticism is hurtful, I appreciate its function. Telling her I understand her difficult predicament is staying engaged. Kathy respecting my self-protection despite its costs is letting me know I'm not doing something wrong. Naming the negative cycle is the first step toward replacing it with a positive cycle.

An easy way to assess if you and your partner are uniting around difficult topics is to notice if either of you is using the word *but*. Typically, *but* is saying, "I need you to understand my perspective because my truth is more important than yours." The *but* is usually a sign of competition; both partners are jockeying for position. If a couple replaces *but* with *and*, they are explicitly stating their intentions to hold two truths simultaneously. Telling Kathy I understand why she comes toward me to talk *and* why I want to go away is holding on to two perspectives. The *and* allows us to bridge our two different realities, a reframing strategy that creates an environment for listening to emotional signals and reaching toward our partner.

We can change self-protective conversations with our partner to more vulnerable ones. If we can expand the tunnel vision of self-protection to include the sharing of underlying needs, then a whole new conversation is possible. Instead of the stress causing more fighting and distance, it can essentially be a harbinger for deeper intimacy. If Kathy empathizes with my fears of failing and responds to me with love when I am in these darker, doubting places, then I can experience the true power of connection. Receiving love in my failing dramatically reduces the pressure to get it right in order to feel safe. This is the best way to teach my body the value of engaging. For Kathy, imagine the different outcome if I comfort her in her anxiety with a hug instead of exacerbating it with distance. Sharing her fears of rejection empowers me to get on my horse and ride to rescue my damsel in distress. The more I respond, the calmer she gets. The calmer she is, the more she tells me I'm getting it right. As the positive cycle grows, so our connection strengthens.

Recognizing a negative cycle of defense and replacing it with a positive cycle of turning toward each other guarantees a strong, resilient bond.

We all hold the keys to our partner's prison. You cannot clap with one hand, and you cannot alter a negative cycle by yourself. Think about a couple where the wife constantly talks and the husband rarely says a word. She wants him to converse more frequently, while he is praying for her to shut up. To change this pattern, he cannot talk more if she doesn't give him some room by talking less. Yet if she gives him space, and he doesn't take it, she is pulled right back into complaining. Too much "me" leaves little room for "we." Working together is the only way toward a healthy, reciprocal, safe connection.

Sex and Stress

One of the greatest gifts we enjoy in relationship is sex. Two people join together to share a pleasurable, bonding moment, which fulfills a universal longing. Given this natural desire for excitement and connection, humans seek fulfillment through sexual intimacy. Sexual intimacy is much more than just a physical release. Sex is the ultimate vehicle for connection.

Studies show that sex is beneficial for your immune system, heart, blood pressure, and sleep and aids in reducing the risk of cancer, reducing pain, relieving stress, improving your relationship, boosting self-esteem, and burning calories through exercise.[19] With advantages like these, why is so much stress attached to sex? Stress enters the picture because sex involves vulnerability. It combines the highs of ultimate acceptance and enjoyment with the lows of failure and rejection.

Popular opinion says that stress is bad for sex. A host of factors such as medical conditions, genetics, overall health, and psychological states contribute to sexual dysfunction. The most common sexual problems are greatly impacted by distress. When we are flooded with stress hormones such as cortisol, it is very challenging to relax and desire sex. Well-known sex therapist Laura Berman says, "Stress makes you tired, distracted and unmotivated to do anything, much less have sex."[20]

Research indicates that 10 to 52 percent of men and 25 to 65 percent of women experience sexual problems.[21] According to a recent survey, 49 percent of women and 37 percent of men say stress is the most significant factor killing their desire for sex.[22] Sadly 15 to 20 percent of couples define their marriage as sexless.[23] Sex is designed to foster connection and security, yet for many it is only adding distress and disconnection. Sex is intended to reduce pressure, not to build it.

Turning toward each other, instead of away, is the first step toward healing. John Gottman, the renowned couples researcher, tells an amusing story about porcupines having sex. The male porcupine faces a unique challenge. To mount his partner from behind, her porcupine needles need to lie down, otherwise, he faces mortal danger. In order to achieve this end, the male faces the female, looks into her eyes, and gently rubs her face with his hands. This emotional connection calms the female to open up and lower her needles.[24] The process is not so different for humans.

Thinking about Sexual Stress Differently

If we learn to use stress as a means to connect, then it leads to a very different outcome. An emphasis on physical functioning or dysfunction misses sex's essential nature: to foster connection. We hope to liberate couples from the pressures of sexual performance by integrating emotional and spiritual components. Our mentor Sue Johnson, the founder of EFT, believes sex without emotion is like trying to dance without music. If the music dies, the dancing is perfunctory and boring. Seeing sexuality within the context of a greater intimate relationship allows for more expression of desire, playfulness, and love. It also allows for the sharing of doubts, fears, and insecurities. Returning the music of emotions to sex allows partners to attune to each other and synchronize their movements. There is nothing more sexually fulfilling and meaningful than two partners authentically risking and responding to each other.[25]

Sex therapists teach couples to improve their sexual communication through sensate focus exercises. Developed by the pioneering sexual researchers William Masters and Virginia Johnson, sensate focus is a specific set of exercises designed to increase both personal and interpersonal awareness of physical needs.[26] Typically, couples are encouraged to touch each other on every part of their bodies to explore their likes and dislikes. Couples notice what feels good or what doesn't work. The goal is heightening awareness and opening up a whole new range of richer experiences.

Although we appreciate the function of these exercises to increase physical mindfulness, we believe sensate focus needs to be applied much more broadly. The essence of sensate focus is to compel couples to slow down and pay attention to the present moment. Whenever we take the time to be mindful of the here-and-now experience, our bodies point us in the direction of what matters most, the emotional bond. What starts off as something physical, the enjoyment of giving and receiving attention, expands to include emotional, mental, and spiritual components. Two people simultaneously focusing on the same moment are united in a larger whole. Sensate focus taps into our universal craving for coordinating movements on many different levels.

The willingness to put aside time to turn toward our partner is the most important step. There is much to gain from simply deciding to hold and touch. This shift to willingness can alleviate some of the guilt stemming from the lack of desire. At the same time as we change the starting point to willingness instead of desire, we also need to shift our destination. It is much healthier to focus on the easily attainable pleasurable connection rather than the elusive mutual orgasm. The main point of sex is the pleasurable act of connection. We can actually achieve this goal without the big orgasm.

In the groundbreaking study "The Components of Optimal Sexuality," researcher Peggy Kleinplatz and her team discovered the components of great sex that are universal in all couples, regardless of their different backgrounds, histories, or sexual tendencies. Even across cultures, the components of great sex are all about connection, not about a specific physical response. These components are (1) being present in the moment, (2) feeling connected and in synch, (3) deep intimacy, (4) good communication and heightened empathy, (5) authenticity, (6) exploration, (7) vulnerability, and (8) a sense of transcendence. These findings suggest that although there are many different routes to experiencing great sex, the actual experience is very similar across individuals.[27] Great sex requires a mutual responsiveness and coordination.

Susan Johnson writes that during sex, "nonverbal cues, sighs, gaze and touch carry exquisitely coordinated signals. The resulting sense of deep rapport creates a synchrony where emotional, physical, and sexual connection can be integrated. In these moments, emotional safety shapes physical synchrony and physical synchrony embodies emotional safety."[28] Sex is intended to be more than just good sensations; it is designed to be a bonding activity. Just imagine the increased vibrancy in our sex lives if we focus on the whole interaction. Helping couples pay attention to their emotional bond is the surest remedy to sexual dysfunction. Let's take a look at the ideal conditions for the best sex.

Great Sex in Marriage

This may be shocking to some readers, but statistics reveal married people enjoy the best sex. Numerous studies find married people have more sex and more varied sex than single people. One of the most widespread studies on sex by the Center for Sexual Health Promotion at Indiana University reported 61 percent of singles had not had sex within the past year, compared with 18 percent of married folk. As for frequency, the study found 5 percent of singles have sex two to three times a week compared to 25 percent of married people.[29]

According to a surprising national study conducted by condom manufacturer Durex, the best sex occurs between people in loving relationships. Their research shows that when partners trust and feel safe, they are confident to try new things. Astonishingly, 96 percent of men and women believe that sex is more fulfilling when there is an emotional connection.[30] This seems to suggest that the anonymous, no-strings-attached sex isn't actually the hottest sex on the planet. Despite the propaganda of

Hollywood, most people's intuition and common sense tells them what is most important for good sex. It turns out that when a partner knows what his or her spouse wants, that knowledge creates a confidence to take risks. The opposite is also true: anxiety and avoidance are linked with fewer positive and more negative feelings during sex.[31] The Durex study concluded that couples who appreciate their emotional connection are more satisfied with their overall sex life, more confident in their sexual prowess, have stronger desires, and are more open to exploration and sexual conversations.

As we observed above, the best sex happens between partners who share loving, honest bonds, which develop and strengthen when the partners repeatedly coordinate movements and adjust to feedback. This attunement is most efficiently accomplished in committed relationships, not in one-night stands or affairs. Sex isn't just a physical union; it also encompasses our universal longing to be known and accepted. When our deepest core is seen and loved, trust grows and we blossom. Trust is the key to focusing our attention in the immediate moment and delivering the heights of sexual pleasure.

Further proof of the value of trust in satisfying sex is the hormone oxytocin. Nicknamed the "love drug," "bliss hormone," and "cuddle hormone," oxytocin is released during moments of connection. Interestingly, oxytocin is also released during the stress response because it is a natural anti-inflammatory that helps us stay relaxed during stress. However, the most important function of oxytocin is to prime us to reach out to family and friends for support. This can occur in a wide range of relational experiences, such as during breastfeeding, friendship, marriage, and orgasm. Oxytocin is most commonly released when physical touch combines with feelings of safety and trust. Scientists tell us oxytocin calms us down and makes us more accepting of others.[32] When we are hugging, kissing, and making love, our bodies need to relax and open up. Biologically, oxytocin helps cement the emotional bond during sex. Obviously, this link between good sex and the need for a trusting bond is wired into our DNA.

We believe the best way to defend the benefits of a committed emotional bond is to emphasize what works best in relationships. This strategy is captured perfectly by a Catholic priest who said, "Porn is not bad because of what it shows but because of what is missing."[33] Reducing sex to a physical activity cheats us of its intended glory. Sex is not meant to be an external act but rather an internal bonding event.

Moving Toward a Deeper Connection

Ideally, marriage and committed relationships are a place for support where two people hold each other up. However, vows are hard to maintain as time and life circumstances pull us away from one another. Intimate relationships demand attention, and without it, sexual problems are a natural by-product.

Sexual stress, like all forms of stress, can be a positive relational builder for those willing to embrace vulnerability as an entrance to connection. Expanding our thinking about what makes for good sex is only one tool for transforming stress in sexual relationships. The other is using the dark corners of sexual dysfunction as a doorway into deeper vulnerability and connection. Although it is often counterintuitive, embracing the darkness can lead us to the light. For couples willing to embrace feedback, the stress of dysfunction can result in deeper attunement and closeness.

Shifting away from an individual's sexual problem to relational issues is a big move toward healing and repair. It is easier to do than most people think. We just need to listen to the distress behind our spouse's complaints—not just to the surface words we typically react to, but to the subtext present in every disagreement. Hearing the story beneath the story allows us to see our spouse as someone who is struggling and needs our grace, just as we need his or her grace. The key is not tuning out the emotional signal but sharing this signal with a responsive partner.

Baring ourselves physically, mentally, emotionally, and spiritually opens up a space to go deeper and help each other understand the good reasons we turn toward unhealthy things to meet our needs. What are we looking for in turning toward pornography, affairs, or a bag of potato chips? Is your partner turning to online sex sites because there is no pressure to perform or fears of rejection? The old Irish saying, "Everyone focuses on the drinking [alcohol] but not the thirst," captures the importance of being curious about what drives our behaviors. Vulnerable partners can explore the thirst together and find healthier ways to quench the dryness. If your partner can turn toward you with his or her fears and darkness, then the distress becomes the impetus for deeper intimacy. Loving your partner in his or her broken places is the surest way to shore up the emotional bond and transform distress into eustress.

Sex and Spirituality

An often quoted piece of marriage advice, sometimes attributed to C. S. Lewis, is that the reason we look for fulfillment outside our own marriage is that we do not allow God to show us the depths of happiness and satisfaction that God can provide in our existing relationship.[34] God's plan for marriage is great sex and mutual adoration. Sex in a healthy, life-giving context can give us a window into an understanding of the human-divine connection. For many mystics across traditions, the soul's ascent is into a state of union or oneness with God. This sacred longing for connection is realized in the act of lovemaking. Many people describing great sex use words normally associated with transcendent spiritual experiences like timelessness, epiphany, transformation, peace, bliss, and ecstasy.[35] Through deep connection we get a felt sense of the eternal. Emphasizing the importance of the emotional bond during sex honors our spiritual heritage and adds the essential missing ingredient necessary to restore sex to its fullest potential.

Without upholding the importance of trust and connection, we are left with inadequate replacements for all that sex is intended to be. Our culture's overemphasis on sexual mechanics, physiology, and performance separates the body from the spirit in sexuality and in the process leaves out the best part, the emotional bond. Whenever the body is cut off from higher aspirations for connection, it is relegated to chasing false substitutes.

Sometimes sexual fantasies can take our focus away from creating a secure connection. Certainly for some couples who share their fantasies within the safety of their bond the added stimulation brings playfulness and strengthens their connection. However, what many people don't realize is that certain images of people and things outside of our relationship that we use to get turned on can actually leave lasting marks on our brain, heart, and body. The intense stimulus creates memories that crave additional stimulation. What starts out as playful curiosity can lead to a compulsion that draws us away from the present moment with our partner. Many people never realize that the porn they are watching may be creating barriers to relational intimacy. Fantasizing about another person to increase arousal while making love to your partner doesn't bridge connection. Quite the contrary, it increases the chasm and exacerbates distress. Figuring out if a fantasy is strengthening the bond or causing disconnection is the easiest way to determine if it enhances or detracts from the health of your marriage.

Ultimately, we believe to restore a healthy perspective on sexuality we must accentuate the traits found in all successful relationships. Our hunger for connection and passionate sex isn't the problem; it is how we fulfill our appetite that matters. Every human being—regardless of gender, race, religion, ethnicity, or sexual orientation—longs to attach, and those with the strongest emotional bonds experience the best sex. The exciting news is there is something to celebrate that is much better than casual sex or boring, going-through-the-motions sex. In the inspired work *The Theology of the Body*, John Paul II reveals God's model for healthy sexuality. Created in the image of the Trinity, we are designed to be in a communion where we live "for the other." We discover our true essence through being in relationship *with* someone else and *for* someone else.[36] Lovingly giving yourself away leads to infinite receiving. The act of giving is as important to the giver as the receiver because it opens both hearts and strengthens love's purpose to continuously circle back and reinforce more sharing.

Sex is the ultimate act of two literally becoming one flesh. The Bible has plenty of examples of passionate sex where the focus is on fostering a bond. For example, Proverbs 5:18–19 says, "May your fountain be blessed, and may you rejoice in the wife of your youth. A loving doe, a graceful deer—may her breasts satisfy you always, may you ever be captivated by her love" (New International Version). "Ever captivated" is all about enjoying the endless benefits of a constantly growing emotional bond.

Healthy sex grows relationships. Our measuring stick for evaluating the health of a sexual act is assessing if the sexual act fosters greater connection or not. Investigating our mysterious sexual energies through innovative methods in the safety of our emotional bond is a good template for healthy sex. Conversely, recreational sex or self-gratification, which lacks the safety of the bond, inevitably leads to a constriction of sexual potential. The secure bond is the natural playground for adventure. It is the bond that sets us free to explore. Anyone experiencing the ecstasy of lovemaking knows she is tapping into something sacred. In connection, there is no worry about the past or future, only the aliveness of the immediate instance, and we believe the best place to meet one another is in the radiant reality of the present moment.

Tying It Together

Long-term relationships are difficult and stress certainly exacerbates negative cycles. If distress takes over relationships, the prognosis is grim. The great news is there is a clear way out of the gloom and away from the scary statistics. Understanding the predictable ways stress triggers our self-protection empowers us to take charge of our actions.

Stress provides the raw materials for change. How we use these materials determines the quality of the product. If we develop a positive attitude about stress in our relationships, it can move us toward a life-giving connection, full of authenticity, openness, and transparency. The mythical problem-free relationship is missing something indispensable. Often it is through the pain, doubt, mistrust, and darkness that we receive healing. Stress opens the doorway into deeper intimacy if we are courageous enough to walk through. Stress shared with your partner invites vulnerability, which is the language of strong connections. We need the messiness of distress to keep fine-tuning the emotional bond. The actual behaviors and dysfunctions are far less important than the intent of the couple to turn toward each other. Lack of connection is a signal to repair our bond. Allowing stress to move us toward our partner and connection transforms the problems into intimacy. In the arms of our secure lover, compassion wins over fear.

CHAPTER 5

Enjoying the Wild Ride

Parenting and Stress

In the movie *Parenthood* (1989) with Steve Martin, the closing scene depicts his child's school play falling apart onstage as Martin sits helplessly in the audience, unable to stop the bedlam. As his stress mounts and the stage set breaks apart, so does his hope for his child's successful performance. In that moment, he senses the rush and twists of a rollercoaster ride. The mysterious words of his mother-in-law about riding a roller coaster suddenly make sense. She had once told him:

> I always wanted to go again. You know, it was just so interesting to me that a ride could make me so frightened, so scared, so sick, so excited, and so thrilled all together! Some didn't like it. They went on the merry-go-round. That just goes around. Nothing. I like the roller coaster. You get more out of it.[1]

Steve had thought she was showing signs of senility, but as he watched the catastrophe onstage, he heard the wisdom in her words. Parenting, like life, is exhilarating if we embrace the chaos and release ourselves from trying to control it. Sitting in that audience while the play fell apart, Martin's character's anxiety melted away as he laughed with abandon.

This metaphor of a wild ride comes to mind when we think about our own parenting struggles or sit across from families trying to find ways to navigate life's challenges together. Although parenting certainly brings great joy and excitement, it can also be a source of enormous pain and confusion.

Parenting is definitely one of the most demanding and rewarding jobs on the planet. The list of challenges is endless and the pay stinks. Yet for the vast majority of parents, they can't even imagine life without their kids. Regardless of the daily grind, being a parent to our kids is one of the best parts of our lives.

Stress challenges all families, and it is the responsibility of parents to model healthy ways of dealing with stress. As parents, how you choose to respond to stress informs your child's perspective. Our children follow our lead and learn to either embrace or avoid stress. It is vitally important for parents to consciously share with their kids a comprehensive map for managing stress. Family members working together off the same map have a much better chance of seeing stress as a challenge the whole family can face together.

If we don't talk to our kids about our strategy for managing stress then we are modeling avoidance and passing along a limited view of stress as something bad to be tolerated. We can do better than just endure stress; we can actually learn to welcome it as an instrument for growth and thriving. Our children deserve a flexible and expansive game plan that sets them up for success. The choice we make as parents goes a long way in determining if our children believe stress is a catalyst for isolation and confusion or connection and clarity.

Families Handling Stress Poorly

Unfortunately, too many parents valiantly attempt to shield their kids from stress by not talking about it. Yet, given the overwhelming amounts of stress in everyday life, this protective approach often only guarantees separated family members must deal with the stress in isolation.

Statistics paint a scary picture about how stressed out families are today. A Harris Poll in August 2014 found 77 percent of parents said parenthood was stressing them.[2] Similarly, according to the American Psychological Association's 2015 report, "Stress in America," parents score higher levels of stress than nonparents in every category: sleeplessness, eating too much or skipping meals, feeling irritable and angry, feeling overwhelmed, and being anxious.[3] Despite the overwhelming distress, the majority of parents don't think their children are strongly affected by it. Nearly three-quarters of parents say their stress has only a slight or no impact on their children.[4] They believe their game plan of hiding distress is working well.

According to their children, however, the game plan is failing dismally. Ninety-one percent of children report they believe their parents are stressed out because it comes out in their yelling, arguing, and complaining.[5] Mixed messages, where the words say "all is good" while the actions say "we are stressed-out," create confusion, chaos, and uncertainty. They can see by our behavior when we are not OK, but they also see that it is not OK to talk about distress.

As we mentioned earlier, stress is very contagious to everyone—but it especially affects children. They are like sponges soaking up signals. According to David Code, author of *Kids Pick Up on Everything: How Parental Stress Is Toxic to Kids,* excessive parental stress is linked to many health problems impacting children today: everything from asthma, diabetes, and allergies to ADHD, autism, and learning disorders are linked to the stress levels of their parents.[6]

Persistent distress is certainly hurting our children's brains. In *Why Zebras Don't Get Ulcers,* psychologist Robert Sapolsky explains how chronic stress interferes with learning and the creation of new neural pathways.[7] Numerous studies reveal children exposed to too much stress have significantly lower IQs.[8] A University of Wisconsin study comparing DNA strands of children found those with stressed-out parents had more negative changes in their DNA than children of calmer parents.[9] Stress actually changes the expression of our DNA by turning on or turning off genes, and these modifications are passed down to future generations. The distress our kids are experiencing today can be passed forward into our molecular heritage.

A host of additional statistics suggest that American children are indeed experiencing stress at new levels: suicides among adolescents have quadrupled since the 1950s; five times more young people are dealing with anxiety and mental health issues today than during the stressful Great

Depression; only 36 percent of seventh graders agreed with the statement "I am happy with my life"; and in the past decade, the use of pharmaceuticals to treat emotional disorders has shot up 68 percent for girls, 30 percent for boys.[10] Sadly, stress is wreaking havoc on our children's physical, emotional, psychological, and spiritual health. In our therapy offices, we are barraged with families overcome with distress.

As professionals teaching others how to handle stress well, we assumed, like most parents, that our own children are the exception and they are handling stress well. Imagine our surprise when we asked our children to rate on a 1-to-10 scale (1 equals no stress, 10 is max-out stress) the amount of stress in their daily lives, and they responded with an average rating of 7.5 to 8. That is way too much distress on a daily basis for healthy development. If our kids believe they are stressed out, then their bodies are negatively impacted by distress. Obviously, we need to do something differently with our children if we hope to enhance their ability to succeed with stress.

Good-Enough Parenting

As we've established, some stress is healthy. It can challenge us to be our best. It is when it moves from healthy stress to unhealthy distress that we need to take care of ourselves and our families. We know how important parenting is, and most of us long to do it better, to find support for our challenging roles, and maybe even some freedom from our distress to assist our children with their own. Considering what standards we hold ourselves to in our parenting can help us identify areas for growth and change for ourselves and our families.

Parents' recognition of their own individual strategies for handling stress is a necessary first step toward modeling effective stress management. Practicing healthy ways of showing the benefits of stress is vital to our children's success. Kids believe what they see: if they see that those around them are stressed out, they won't trust admonishments not to stress.

I (Heather) am the mother of a thirteen-year-old daughter and stepmother to a twenty-two-year-old daughter and a twenty-five-year-old son. I am a learner, a mom who gets it right on the good days and falls miserably short on the bad ones. I am doing the best I can as a working mom, striving to integrate a blended family. I daily pray for grace, strength, and wisdom. We live in the suburbs of New York City. Like most communities today outside big cities, the bar is high for children and adults to succeed and thereby fit in. I grew up in this area and know people notice the type of car your family drives, where you go on vacation, what clothes you wear, and whether you party or not. Helping my daughter with college applications, I realized that growing up here you need to be well rounded, play sports, and do service and community work. These are all things that matter if you want to get into the top schools.

Wanting to do our best as parents, we often confuse helping our children become healthy and responsible adults with sheltering them from hurt and harm in a world that seems anxious to force them to grow up too fast. When most of our children's peers are on several sports teams or taking on extracurricular activities to get ahead, we may feel we are doing a disservice to not help them keep up with others in a race to the top. Many parents feel these pressures even when their children are preschoolers.

How will we teach our children that they are good enough as themselves and don't need to perform and get ahead (or get all As) to be loved and accepted? This is especially difficult to teach if we hold ourselves to the adult version of these expectations. Pressure takes its toll on everyone. Finding ways to reduce distress is critical to establishing healthier family dynamics.

I frequently talk to parents who are anxious to find a "less stressed" way of living and raising families. Reframing stress as necessary and healthy goes a long way in changing its impact from negative to constructive. Our children need to know that stress is our friend, not the big bad bully. If we believe stress is unhealthy, it is unhealthy. We wonder why overwhelmed kids lack drive. Distress crushes hope and replaces it with resignation. Children need parents to teach them the benefits of stress so they can hold on to their hopes.

To teach their children to think differently, parents also need to know how to reduce distress and increase eustress in their own lives. As we mentioned in chapter 5, turning toward your partner for support is a great way to turn distress into eustress. Even if parents can't change the circumstance, being in it together makes a huge difference. Roger Kobak and Toni Mandelbaum's in their paper "Caring for the Caregiver: An

Attachment Approach to Assessment and Treatment of Child Problems" found that positive change in families is most likely to occur when one parent becomes more confident in the availability of his or her partner.[11] The key to attuned, effective parenting is a secure alliance between parents. Partners who decide to stand together to raise children create a dramatically different environment from those who blame each other.

The concept of "good-enough parenting" from psychology provides a major relief valve that allows parents to exhale and begin to relax. One study that is particularly encouraging for parents found that "the best caregivers correctly respond to their child's need for love and support only about 50 percent of the time."[12] Parents have good reasons to miss signals and fail to respond. There are times when parents feel tired or distracted. The telephone rings or there is breakfast to prepare. Despite the best of intentions, parents' communications are either out of synch or misattuned. For example, a parent gives a hug when the child wants advice to fix something, or the parent gives advice when the child just needs a hug. Life makes demands on all of us, and we have to attend to them, which at times means we are not good listeners or communicators. Other issues or people require our attention. Misses and ruptures are par for the course in all relationships.

Another researcher, Ed Tronick, director of UMass Boston's Infant-Parent Mental Health Program, suggests the best parents are only perfectly in synch with their child 30 percent of the time. The other 70 percent of the time they are out of synch and trying to get back in synch.[13] Getting back into synchrony is the crucial process: it is repairing a breakdown in the connection between two individuals and returning them to a state of relational harmony. Each time a relationship is restored, it is even stronger than before the original rupture because both people involved are now confident that breakdowns can be fixed. The process of connecting and disconnecting (or misattunement) is normal and to be expected—and even necessary. Teaching our children how to repair relationships—and not necessarily to be perfect—is essential to healthy development. There are many times as parents that we try to intervene on our children's behalf but miss what they are really saying, which results in annoying or disturbing them. Imagine how relieving it is for children to witness their parents' modeling repair by saying, "I'm sorry, my good intentions didn't work very well." Instead of disregarding their irritation as unnecessary, how different it could be if we acknowledged how the misattunement wasn't what they needed. Then the very miss becomes the source of connection.

There is so much pressure on parents to be perfect. These percentages may be a lot lower than what we often hold ourselves to. Do you feel bad with every missed connection or disagreement? What do you think of getting parenting right only between 30 and 50 percent of the time? Are you surprised that is good enough? We hope this perspective takes some pressure off you as parents. When we get it right that is awesome, and when we get it wrong that, too, is OK, as long as we know how to repair.

The wisdom "I am enough, I have enough, I do enough" is on the Workaholics Anonymous list of Affirmations.[14] We don't know about you, but we find those words incredibly freeing. It challenges our false beliefs that we need more, we are not good enough, and that we need to earn love and worthiness. It reminds us to relax, take a deep breath, and receive the moment. Parents often measure their performance against unattainable standards. Instead, what if we ended each day with a prayer of thanks that today was enough?

Sometimes we have to do our best and, at the end of the day, accept our limitations. One psychoanalyst, Karen Horney, believed we must all accept "the ordinariness of one's real self."[15] From the *I Ching: Points of Balance and Cycles of Change* by Peggy Jones, we hear this wisdom restated: "We need to remain quietly in touch with our ordinariness."[16] This is hard for us. How about for you? A wise friend shared with us many years ago this tidbit: "All we are called by God to do is offer the small cup of water we have been given despite the ocean of need that may surround us.[17] We are not superwomen or supermen as much as we like to believe we are. We are asked to be faithful with what we have been given. That is good enough.

A Map to Effective Parenting

The essence of good-enough parenting is meeting the basic emotional needs of children, providing a balance of both love and structure. Children need emotional connection to feel safe. Yet children also need structure, order, and predictability so they can feel secure. Boundaries help children to establish a sense of self and other and to learn how to function in a world that will not always respond to their whims. Effective parents know that true love is both nurture and limit.

The Importance of Emotional Connection

Finding the right balance is often difficult. Many parents in previous generations focused more on structure than love. They excelled at providing clear boundaries, discipline, and limits. Kids knew their place, and the rules were explicit. Unfortunately, too much focus on the rules left many kids feeling unimportant, invisible, and unloved. We both remember some of our grandparents who wanted us "to be seen but not heard." We believed our grandparents didn't like us. It is hard to feel important when there is little opportunity to emotionally engage.

Too much structure and not enough emotional support leads to a rigid and sterile environment where order is solid but connections are weak. Parents need to raise, nurture, and train up, but also connect with their children. The most powerful force on this planet is connection. Connection is the pathway toward love, joy, peace, comfort, satisfaction, and health. In parenting, we don't have to be rich or smart or talented or funny. We just have to be there.[18]

Brené Brown wrote, "Connection is why we are here. Each of us needs to know we are worthy of love and belonging. Part of how we cultivate connection is through vulnerability."[19] There is something risky about loving and being open. We can do that only if we model taking care of ourselves and turning to others for support, if we are willing to fail and say we're sorry, to repair the connection when it is broken.

As a parent, I (Heather) confess that at times I don't always handle my child's anger or hurt as well as I could. On good days, I try to listen to her heart and what her behavior is saying. If she is distressed by her day at school and overtired, a barrage of energy may be directed at me. I try to remember not to take it personally. It may be hard for me to hear what happened to her in school: a friend hurt her, a teacher disappointed her, she didn't make the team. I want to avoid her hurt and sadness as much as I do my own, but a wonderful opportunity for deeper connection awaits both of us as we lean into those emotions together.

However, we know that the best gift we can give our children is our presence. That means to listen deeply and not try to repair, fix, or correct the problem but to walk in our children's shoes, to "get" them, and even admit sometimes we don't know what to say, but regardless, we are thankful for their sharing. Happiness shared multiplies, while expressing sorrow with another divides the pain. The goal is to be in whatever circumstances life brings us together. A helpful tool for parents to enhance their connection is to try to match the affect or emotion of their child. It is easier for two brains to connect when the emotional states are similar. For example, if a child is excited or upset telling a story and his parent responds in a calm, detached manner, the child likely will shut down or get frustrated. The misattunement leads the child to believe that his parent "doesn't get it." Instead, if the parent raises his energy to join in the excitement, the child is much more likely to continue. The parent's attunement sends clear signals that he can see how much this impacts his child, and they are sharing in their passion.

If your kids are animated about something and you respond to them with flat comments, see how quickly their balloon deflates. There is nothing like misattuned energy to create distance in relationships. However, if you respond with matched excitement, see how their balloon expands. The air in our balloons often comes from those inhaling or exhaling around us.

I (George) tried mirroring my son's emotions one night when I was practicing shooting basketballs with him. Dylan is an excellent athlete, and he expects to perform well. This particular night, none of his shots were going into the basket. As he continued to miss shots, his frustration mounted. Finally, after missing another shot, he threw the basketball away, shouting, "I hate basketball! It sucks! I never want to play it again!" Here was one of those moments parents dread. What to do? Should I do what my father did to me, which was to say, "Stop your whining! If you want to make the shot, bend your knees and follow through with your hand."

If you could have gotten inside Dylan's brain during the meltdown, you would have discovered the strong emotions were actually overwhelming his ability to take in information. Advice just wouldn't get through to him. It was not his choice to disregard any advice; his brain just couldn't process it in the moment of dysregulation. I easily could have made matters worse. When Dylan rejects my attempts to help, I typically get frustrated with his "disrespectful behavior" and react with my own anger. We both fall into a predictable negative pattern of anger fueling anger.

Most of the time I get it wrong with my misattuned advice, but this night I tried something new. I ran after the basketball, picked it up, and started to punch it saying, "Bad basketball! Bad basketball! I hate you to. Stop being so difficult or I'm going to pop you!"

Guess what my son Dylan did when he watched my crazy behavior? He started to laugh. What did the laughter do? It started to calm and soothe his brain. Then a fascinating thing happened. Dylan turned to me and asked for advice on making the shot. Wow! Dylan never asks for advice. I even ask other dads to point things out to him because he doesn't want to listen to me. But in a shared moment of laughter and connection, he felt safe to ask for help.

Another good strategy is to limit the questions and lectures. Questions add a sense of evaluation that kids want to avoid. Before a parent even finishes asking a question, her child's body is bracing for something uncomfortable to happen. Kids often don't see a question as an invitation to connect but rather as an accusation to defend against. The last thing overwhelmed kids want to deal with is more judgment and evaluation. It is more effective for parents to show their interest by making authentic comments. For example, instead of asking, "How was school today?" which elicits the universal response, "Fine," try initiating a conversation by saying something like, "My day was pretty boring except for this one thing . . ." If your child is interested in knowing more, she will respond. If she chooses to disengage, try again later.

Because availability and being present are the key factors in connection, we parents need to keep asking ourselves, "How much are we on our cell phones or computers when they are trying to talk to us?" Good parenting requires self-reflection and honest appraisal. A cartoon we often use during our parenting trainings is a picture of a parent reading a book at the beach about how to be a better parent while his child is bugging him to play and he is too busy to engage. Our kids, like our partners, know when we are focused on them or distracted and semi-listening. If we are open to their feedback then it provides an invitation for us to do better, try again, repair a breach in the connection, and get back into synchrony. Let us not lose the opportunity in our children asking more from us.

We usually have good reasons for missing the mark. I (George) remember sitting with a mother in my therapy room, waiting for her seven-year-old daughter to join us for a family session. We were watching the little girl play with a big dog outside. The girl and the dog were jumping around and thoroughly enjoying each other's company. The mom and I had huge smiles on our faces as we delighted in their exuberant connection. When the girl walked into our room, though, her mother communicated a reaction very different from that enjoyment. The little girl didn't get the smile but instead received a shaking head and comments on her dirty dress. Mom had a valid intention—to help her daughter maintain a decent appearance—but she failed to connect with her daughter. The mother's response was in stark contrast to the dog's, the girl's recent playmate. He was ready to join her to play in the moment. Dogs seem better at enjoying the benefits of connection than we are. Most groups we have spoken to in the past resonate with this saying, "I wish I were the person my dog thinks I am." Dogs are available and open for connection and come to us without prejudgment or criticism. They are glad to see us. Don't we want the same from our partners, family members, or parents?

Lack of Discipline

Many baby boomers rebelled at their parents' overemphasis on structure and vowed that their kids would never feel the same pain of rejection and isolation. Some swung too far in the opposite direction. They excelled at providing unconditional love but came up short in the discipline department. But now parents' noble desire to protect and praise their precious children is producing entitled kids who believe the world is here for their pleasure. Everyone gets a trophy regardless of effort. All the emphasis on immediate attention and responsiveness is creating an impatient generation that wants it all now. The overemphasis on comfort and underemphasis on structure results in chaos and insecurity.

We often hear parents complain about how rude, disrespectful, and rebellious their children are. As parents, we need to examine what messages we are sending our children. We can all relate to having a hard day at the office and deciding it is easier to give in rather than have the argument that would prevent the child from getting his own way. It appears easier to be a friend to one's child rather than an authority figure. Giving in seems easier than standing up to or for what is really in the child's best interest, like establishing a reasonable bedtime, refraining from sweets before bed, or finding out if the friend's parents are home for the sleepover. However, the child who seems to demand his way actually doesn't want the power to be in charge. For most children and even teens, being in control is frightening. Without learning limits from the caring adults in their lives, they will not know how to regulate themselves emotionally or behaviorally now or later in life.

When kids lack structure, they often turn to their peers for the missing support. But friends replacing parents as teachers of rules and values typically leads to bad outcomes.[20] Peers lack the wisdom, empathy, and unconditional love necessary to make good role models and disciplinarians. The result of parents' abdication of their responsibilities is an atmosphere of chaos instead of security. Always getting their way makes kids less resilient to face challenges necessary for growth. As life gets harder and these enabled kids struggle, they don't know how to face adversity and throw temper tantrums to express their discomfort. The more out of control the kids feel, the more their parents feel helpless to stop their acting-out behaviors. As the reactivity in the family escalates, kids often find themselves disconnected from both their families and their peers; no one knows what is really going on inside them. The disconnected adolescent fears his parents will not relate because he assumes they will think his problems, like identity issues or peer pressure, aren't a big deal. His friends also may not understand him and may belittle him or try to persuade him to do things he isn't really comfortable with but may feel forced to do to fit in. Peer discipline is harsh, and it can kill vulnerability. Turning to parents or peers without appropriate structure can lead to a lack of support and isolate the adolescent further.

A lack of structure also proves damaging in the future, when children discover they lack the self-discipline to hold down a job, get into and through college, make friendships, and date. Our children need to learn to operate in a social world where others can trust in their ability and willingness to turn in assignments, to tell the truth, to follow through. In our therapy offices, some of the biggest breakthroughs come when parents can see their child's need for clear limits. The appropriate no is just as important as a big hug. A child needs to know her parent is bigger, stronger, and wiser. This trust in her parent's wisdom provides the child protection against the many uncertainties of life. Devoid of such protection, kids are adrift in a sea of worries.

Finding the right balance between love and discipline goes a long way toward creating the safety in homes necessary to teach children how to embrace stress rather than fear it. Making life too easy for children teaches them to avoid discomfort, while making life too hard teaches them to strive for achievement at the expense of connection and vulnerability. Children need healthy adults to model for them how to deal with failure, disappointments, and anger, as well as how to take appropriate risks, weigh choices, and work with what they are given. Again, the best predictor for how children perceive stress is their parents' perception of stress. A sensitive, structured and responsive caregiver provides a "safe base" for exploration and sets a child up for success in dealing with stress. So, parents, keep your love-and-discipline balance by remembering to tell your kids they are perfect the way they are, and when they mess things up you will help them amend their ways. This way we keep our hearts soft and our skin thick.

Recognizing Family Patterns of Protection

In all families, family members fall into predictable patterns to protect themselves when stress strikes. As we discussed in chapter 4 on romantic relationships, there are two typical ways of dealing with stress: pulling away to escape talking about the stress or pushing forward to force a conversation. In couples, it is easy to see how the combination of one person pushing and one person withdrawing creates a vicious feedback loop that reinforces the need for further self-protection from the other person who is seen as causing harm. Let's take a look at a typical family of four and how quickly multiple feedback loops can develop during a simple family dinner together.

Son: I'm finished eating. Can I be excused?

Daughter: Why are you always in a rush to leave?

Son: Shut up and mind your own business.

Daughter: You shut up. Maybe you need to address your anger issues. I don't care anyway; you are a mean jerk.

Dad: OK, stop the fighting. It's OK if he wants to leave.

Daughter: You always take his side. I'm sick of it.

Dad: I'm not taking sides. I just don't like it when you call him a jerk.

Mom: Hey, wait a second. It's not her fault. She only said that after he told her to shut up. They are both wrong.

Dad: Now you're going to jump on me too? You always want me to get involved, and when I do, all I hear is I'm doing it wrong. This is not worth fighting about. I'm going to the family room and turning the game on.

Mom: Right, run away when it gets difficult. What else is new?

As the scene above depicts, in less than a minute, the family cohesion quickly deteriorates into each person feeling isolated. Despite a slew of research indicating the multiple benefits of eating together, many parents question the wisdom of their decision to eat together after so many disastrous outcomes. To avoid fights, many families choose to eat apart most of the time. Unfortunately, as defenses increase to stop the bad things from happening, they also keep out the good stuff. Many families are caught in these negative cycles of protection, and the worst part is they don't even realize it.

These predictable patterns wreak havoc in our relationships whether we are aware of them or not. Most family members get lost talking about surface issues—video games, friends, food, school, money, and sports— and miss the underlying process, which is all about the state of their connection. What really matters is whether they feel seen, understood, respected, and loved. Failure to risk discussing the core issues leaves only the surface topics to argue about.

As family members protect themselves from negative interactions by either withdrawing or protesting, other family members also feel threatened. Like in war, defensiveness breeds additional defensiveness. Look at the interdependency of behaviors in the above example. The brother starts the ball going by wanting to leave, triggering his sister's protests. The brother feels criticized by his sister's protest, which strengthens his desire to pull away. The sister feels rejected by the brother's withdrawal, which fuels her additional protest. The son's propensity to withdraw is very similar to Dad's. The daughter's tendency to criticize is familiar to Mom's strategy. All are employing short-term strategies to deal with the interpersonal stress. Unfortunately these immediate solutions to survive create a feedback loop of further self-protection in every family member. The family's ability to connect, comfort, and repair shrinks with each turn of the negative cycle.

Transforming Distress Through Vulnerability

The home is supposed to be a place of safety and acceptance. If families can identify how defensiveness is creating distance and getting in the way of healthy connections, then there is hope for replacing negative patterns with positive ones. All the misses, defensiveness, and misattunement are opportunities for repair and deeper connection for those willing to vulnerably engage. Bickering during dinner doesn't need to end in disaster. Instead, the fighting can lead to restoration and closeness.

The key to transforming distress into eustress is shifting the conversation from the content on the surface to the emotional signals underneath. Vulnerability pulls others closer, while defensiveness pushes family members away. Let's return to our previous example to see other possible outcomes. Notice each family member has a chance to shift levels and start a vulnerable conversation.

Son: I'm finished eating. Can I be excused?

Daughter: I know you are excited to play your video game, but I haven't spent any time with you. I miss you and feel bad when we get so little time together. I start to worry that you don't want to hang out with me, that I am not cool enough for you.

Son: Wow, I didn't know it bothered you so much. I didn't think you even noticed. I'm sorry you feel sad. It's not going to kill me to hang out a few more minutes. I think you are still cool.

Dad: This is really nice. I really appreciate it when you two are able to talk to each without any bickering.

Mom: What a wonderful meal when we can be together and eat without any tensions.

In this example, the daughter risks expressing her vulnerable feelings, which pulls her brother to engage. His responsiveness to her sadness strengthens their connection. The parents' positive energy is a direct result of witnessing their kids beautifully connecting. Dinner is more enjoyable when our kids are shining instead of fighting. A positive cycle of responsiveness is just as contagious as a negative cycle. When we compare this encounter with the previous example, which ends in separation, what we see almost looks like two totally different families.

Once family members understand cycles, they are each empowered with the ability to shift the levels of communication at any time. In the original example, let's say the brother and sister fail to shift levels and fall into a defensive, negative cycle. Now the ball is in the parents' court to model vulnerability. For example:

Dad: Hey, can we stop the arguing? I'm really looking forward to hanging out with you both and having some fun together. When you two start fighting, I want to make it stop but sometimes no matter what I try, it doesn't work. I don't know what to do. I guess I feel like I'm not doing my job as a dad.

Son: Dad, it is not your fault—you're a great dad. I don't know what to do either.

Daughter: Sorry, Dad. I just asked him to stick around because he can always make me laugh, and I had a bad day. Maybe we can do something after dinner all together?

Mom: (*Smiling.*) OK, let's watch a romantic, tear-jerker movie.

Dad: (*Laughing.*) Just when I thought our night was taking a turn for the better.

There is no perfect, cookie-cutter script; what is needed is just the ability to slow down and share the underlying emotional signals. Dad let his family in on his longing for connection and his fears of disconnection. Again, the vulnerability pulls people toward us, while the self-protection creates distance. As we see with Mom's comment, humor helps shift the energy. We are not helpless victims to the negative cycle; each family member holds the key to transform the negative into a positive interaction.

Remember, perfection isn't the goal. We don't need to get it right all the time, just good enough. Even when we fall back into old habits, repair can happen the next day when things are a bit calmer. Going back to our original example, where the whole family fights and goes off to separate rooms, imagine this conversation the next day at dinner.

Mom:	I think we need to talk about what happened at dinner yesterday. It may sound scary because we all get tense and worry about starting another fight. I know it might be easier to leave than have this talk. But I also know how sad I feel when we can't talk and we all go off to different parts of the house. I see this pattern happening a lot lately. The guys want to avoid talking and the gals want more conversation. But each side makes the other more upset. What do you think we can do differently as a family to get out of this mess?
Son:	Maybe we can compromise. We talk a little more, and you make fewer comments.
Daughter:	I definitely can make fewer comments. I never realized they bothered you so much.
Dad:	I guess we have two pretty smart kids. They must take after their mother.

We know what many of you are thinking when reading these quick transcripts: real families do not talk this way. But these types of conversations do happen; we help families have them all the time. Our experience working with many families is that a positive cycle really is just as likely to result as is a negative cycle for families aware of their underlying attachment needs. According to noted academic Dennis Saleebey, "It is as wrong to deny the possible as it is to deny the problem."[21] It is just as easy for a conversation to pull people together as it is to push them apart. Training ourselves and our children to listen to our emotional signals and share them in a way other members can respond to creates an amazingly healthy environment in which we can all thrive.

To attain these positive conversations, we don't have to be perfect. There is lots of room in families to misattune. If the misattunement is temporary and can be repaired, then it is incredibly healthy and adaptive. We need to get it wrong to know how to get it right. The process of repair is so powerful because embedded in all distress is the prospect for eustress. Families grow with constant adjustment.

Parenting and Spirituality

Stress within families provides endless possibilities to deepen relationships through repair and reconnection. Good parenting, like good spirituality, is all about knowing how to maintain closeness and repairing distance. Most spiritual traditions emphasize the redemptive value of adversity and support the plethora of research accentuating the importance of connection. The Bible provides many stories of repair. On the cross, it was the sinful thief who modeled vulnerability, empathy, remorse, and compassion toward Jesus that led to his salvation. It seems the broken characters like the tax collectors, prostitutes, soldiers, slaves, widows, and beggars who recognize their failures (misattunements), and the need for God's help, are able to discover paradise. Compare the broken characters' ability to connect with God to the Pharisees who strived for perfection but left little room for expressing vulnerability and their need for others. Their drive to appear above reproach, unfortunately, led to disconnection. God wants the church to be, as the saying goes, "a hospital for sinners, not a museum for saints."

Parker Palmer, a noted author and educator, said, "Relational trust is built on movements of the human heart such as empathy, commitment, compassion, patience and the capacity to forgive."[22] Those behaviors go a long way toward helping us find our footing as parents, spouses, children, and friends. They sound like a list from the Christian Scriptures on the fruit of the Spirit, evidence of a life abiding in God, in Galatians 5. Think of people you know with these qualities: love, joy, peace, patience, kindness, generosity, faithfulness, gentleness, and self-control (Gal. 5:22–23). All these "fruits" deepen connection. But being that kind of person is not easy. Most would argue it requires grace and a belief in something greater than ourselves at work in us to achieve. We also need to be able to ask for and give forgiveness to our spouses and children when we don't live up to these fruits. Our honesty and humility is far more important than getting it right. Finding ways to care for ourselves and inviting others into our challenges and triumphs will go a long way toward easing the burden of today's pressures and perfectionism in families.

Children need unconditional love and structure just like they need food and shelter to survive. Many religious communities stress the importance of both good works (structure) and grace (love). Ken Ginsburg, pediatrician and author of *Building Resilience in Children and Teens: Giving Kids Roots and Wings*, writes, "Unconditional love is the bedrock of resilience because it creates security" for children to thrive.[23] Parents are not exempt from this universal need for unconditional love. If parents can gain security from the ultimate source of unconditional love, from God, how much better are they going to be in serving their children? It is not surprising, when we understand the power of connection to reduce distress, to realize that the ability to turn toward God is another powerful relief valve, just like leaning on our spouse.

When we embrace the divine spark of love and hold to the ultimate truth that nothing we do can separate us from God's love, then we are better able to respond to distress. We all doubt at times, but for those willing to follow the pathway of vulnerability, the uncertainties only foster greater intimacy. God always leaves the door open for repair. Parents' sacred task is to teach their children to trust stress as an indispensable component to healthy connection, with each other and with God. Our children definitely notice from where we draw our security and strength.

How we care for ourselves and others is the measure by which our children will listen to our words. If we make rest and play a high priority in our lives and do not just work or consume technology night and day, children can relax and learn to engage others in healthy ways. If we celebrate joyous moments and grieve appropriately when we encounter losses and suffering, they learn there is a rhythm to life that can be respected and that challenges can be tolerated and worked through. Knowing how to handle criticism and work through disagreements in healthy and constructive ways transforms conflict into something tolerable that can be managed for even better outcomes. Do we have the freedom to fail and learn from our mistakes and the grace to forgive ourselves and our loved ones? Do we believe that spiritual support—divine comfort and encouragement and a spiritual family or religious worship community—is available to uphold us in this sacred yet challenging task of parenting? If so, we are living the most persuasive message we could impart to the next generation.

Part 3

How External Realities Shape Our Stress

In the first two parts of this book, we discussed how stress impacts our interior world and the relationships we engage in. In this part, our focus shifts to external stress, which is simply any stress that arises from factors outside our individual experience or interactions with others. Examples of external stressors are economic issues, cultural changes, or traumatic events. External stressors include a wide range of influences that can impact our lives in varying degrees. Every day we face the daily hassles of external stress, such as bad weather, traffic, too much noise, and not enough money or time. Each frustrating event can insidiously chip away at our patience and overall health. In addition, big external events can rock our world in a heartbeat. Think about a car accident, a fire, a crime, an earthquake, a stock-market crash, or a war.

Although there are countless external stresses, we shall focus on two general categories, money and trauma. Both of these external stresses remind us that we aren't in control and live in a world of unpredictability and change. We will consider the physical, emotional, psychological, and spiritual consequences of these stressors on us, knowing that being able to face these challenges with integrity and serenity is vital for health and for making good choices for a full life.

CHAPTER 6

Breaking a Dependency

Handling Money with Integrity

Given the precarious and often unpredictable nature of finances, it is the ideal environment for breeding stress. Most people think (or worry) about money every day. Money is at the heart of so many life decisions and conflicts in our relationships. We have to deal with different ideas about who earns the money, who gets to keep and spend it, and what priorities apply to limited resources. Often the achievement of our goals and dreams is measured in financial success. More money means you can have the house of your dreams, the new car, and the lifestyle of the rich and famous. Every day we are besieged with messages from television, newspapers, the Internet, and the people around us, pressuring us to pursue and spend more money. Personal financial security is equated with opportunity, travel, education, and the ability to pay health-care bills or buy expensive toys.

In our society, we tend to believe that money equals pleasure, while a lack of money equals pain. Given our attraction to comfort and aversion to pain, it makes sense that so many view money as the holy grail. For many people, money becomes the measure of a person's worth. The unrelenting message we receive is money is the key to safety, security, and happiness. But a money-obsessed culture chases a lie. Fighting frantically for a bigger piece of the pie leaves few winners and many losers. The richest one hundred people in the world actually own more wealth than the bottom 3.5 billion people combined.[1] With staggering statistics like this, one thing is certain: those wrestling for the crumbs will face huge amounts of stress.

For individual Americans, money is consistently the number one stressor. Almost three-quarters of Americans say they are stressed about money.[2] Unfortunately, their answer to relieving the stress is to work harder and chase the money even faster, which in turn increases stress, harms relationships, and takes away time for self-care and relationships. The negative feedback loop picks up momentum with each worrisome thought. According to an American Psychological Association report, "financial struggles strain individuals' cognitive abilities, which could lead to poor decision-making and may perpetuate their unfavorable financial and health situations."[3]

In confronting an unhealthy attachment to money, we must examine its core assumption that money is the key to happiness. Studies show that for the past fifty years Americans have been getting richer, but they are not getting any happier.[4] In fact, increased levels of anxiety, depression, mental illness, and suicide are pushing the happiness meter in the wrong direction. The research of Nobel Prize economist Angus Deaton reveals that contrary to what most of us believe, once we have enough income to cover our basic needs, more money does not increase our happiness.[5] Fellow researcher Richard Easterlin's comprehensive study of fifty-four countries found similar results worldwide: there is no long-term relationship between economic growth and happiness.[6] Ed Diener, who has been studying happiness for over thirty years, believes the benefit of having more money is often mitigated by the sacrifices people make to earn the money. Studies have associated higher incomes with increased levels of distress, marital discord, and less enjoyment in activities.[7] Clearly the road to happiness is not paved with gold and dollar bills.

Like the one drink too many or an affair, money seems to give a quick burst of happiness that quickly dissipates as stress from the pressure of working or worrying about having enough replaces feelings of happiness. To make matters worse, the energy we invest in making money can take us away from the essential opportunity of life, connecting with others. Researcher Kathleen Vohs found the more people think about money, the less helpful and the more self-focused, selfish, and isolated they become.[8] It is ironic that trying to find happiness in acquisition can get in the way of securing true satisfaction in relationships. The best things in life cannot be bought; they need to be experienced. Researcher Ryan Howell says that life experiences give us more long-term pleasure than material things, and yet we still deprive ourselves of experiences to buy material things.[9] The pursuit of money warps our perceptions and complicates our needs. Most of us have simpler needs than we think, so perhaps our view of money needs to be expanded.

Expanding How We See Money

As we discuss in every chapter of this book, believing that some kind of stress is unhealthy for us will impact our physical health as well. Too many of us are stressed out over never having enough money, and the chronic distress is reducing the quality of our lives. Expanding our awareness of what is not working in regard to money allows us to find healthier alternatives, thereby turning the distress into eustress. The first step to stopping the distress of money from taking over our lives is to acknowledge there is a problem. Money is not the real problem; it is our motivations and intentions surrounding money that get us into trouble. Our view that money is the panacea for all problems can set us up for failure. It creates an intimate and emotional relationship to money that it simply can't reciprocate or fulfill. Money is an inattentive and unresponsive partner. When we look to money as the thing that makes us feel special, important, and loved, then everything else becomes secondary. Overvaluing money in our hearts tends to result in undervaluing people.

We need to put money in proper perspective. When we develop a mind-set that money is just a tool, a means to an end, we avoid the emotional attachment that gives it so much power. Money is designed for payment of good and services, not to ensure our security or prove we are worth loving. All of us need to honestly assess our relationship with money. Does money provide status or fill a void? Is money what makes you feel safe? If the answers to these questions are yes, then money is in control of your life. Like an addict hooked on a drug, we are letting money run the show. We can take back control from money by attaching our emotional needs to healthier objects, like others or God.

If every day we worry about money and believe it is the answer to our problems, we strengthen those neural pathways in our brains that maintain our enchantment with the false promise. The key to changing this unhealthy relationship to money is recognizing our dependency. When we find ourselves thinking, "Owning this new car will impress everyone," we need to acknowledge the normal insecurities driving the desire. By doing so, we break our dependency on money and find healthier ways to meet our underlying needs. Every time we feel distress about money, we can remind ourselves, "Regardless of whether I have enough money, I'm still blessed to have time to be around those people I love." Spending time connecting with those who enjoy being around us can combat the insecurity that propels us to impress people by having a nice car. We retrain our minds when using our financial concerns as reminders of what really matters and spend time with those who make us feel secure. This is another way we can turn distress into eustress. After all, the best investment we can make with our money is to spend it in experiences or save or invest it on behalf of our relationships.

O. Henry's story "The Gift of the Magi" is a powerful illustration of how love trumps monetary concerns and puts everything into a healthier perspective. In the story, a young couple, Jim and Della, are struggling to make ends meet. They possess nothing of value except for Jim's gold watch, passed down from his father, and Della's beautiful, long hair. Each wants to buy a Christmas present for the other but lacks the money. In their desperation to get a gift for each other, Jim sells his watch to buy Della accessories for her beautiful hair, and Della sells her hair to buy Jim a chain for his watch. On a practical level, their gifts now are useless, but that misses the deeper truth. Each partner's willingness to sacrifice for the other reminds them both how priceless their love really is. Although they have real money problems, these problems pale in comparison to their gratitude for that which they do possess. Honoring our connections puts money in a limited, secondary role, which is where it belongs. This awareness can bring much healing into our world.

Think about how much less stress we can all have in our lives if we develop a healthy relationship with money and learn to steward our resources wisely. When we are liberated from addictive, emotional attachments to money, we can use it more effectively. We can do a lot of good with money when we use it as intended, to pay for goods and services and to open doors for others' advancement and not to meet our security needs. Giving to charity shifts our focus back to the importance of helping others. The research is crystal clear: giving makes us happy, stimulating the areas of the brain associated with pleasure, social connection, and trust.[10] Activities that enhance connection always create joy. The more we associate money with helping relationships, the more money becomes a vehicle for eustress. Expanding our view about money from one of personal gain to collective good is powerful and positive. Like all forms of stress, eustress is contagious and grows as people catch a shared vision of using our limited resources for the greater good of those we love and the world. Imagine how different our world might be if most used money in life-giving ways.

Turning Toward Connection

Shifting our thinking about money is one way to reduce its negative impact. The second path is leaning into our emotional signals regarding money. Given that we often have a misplaced emotional attachment to money, it is understandable why bringing up the topic is charged with emotion and can lead to disagreements and disconnection. Many people talk about money only when absolutely necessary. This strategy of avoidance inevitably creates distance and mistrust, leaving each person alone to guess the other's intentions. Despite the challenges of discussing money, in every relationship—parent-child, roommates, couples, families, colleagues, or friends—each conversation about money is an opportunity for further closeness once challenges and differences are worked through. When one person honors and recognizes the deeper significance of money for the other, he can hear and respond to the other better. No two people are going to see any topic exactly alike. In working through differences, we have the chance to be vulnerable with one another, to learn something new, and to grow closer through the exchange.

When we find ourselves stressed by money, our worry should be a signal to us, reminding us to be curious. Once we start listening to our feelings, or emotional signals, about money, we can use that information to communicate our needs. To demonstrate, let's take a look at a typical couple that walks into our office.

Sarah grew up with a father who was a gambler. He managed to hold down a decent job but used up the family funds on his addiction. Her childhood felt chaotic. She never knew if there would be extra spending money, or even a new winter coat and boots, because her dad's behavior varied from month to month. She witnessed her mom complaining day after day but saw no change in her dad's behavior or their family's financial security. This experience deeply affected her relationship with money. Sarah committed herself to always being responsible with money.

Todd grew up in a privileged community and is used to having the best of everything, whether it is clothes, sports equipment, cars, or zip codes. He is working in his family's business, although not overly compensated as he is working his way up the ranks to assume future leadership.

Fast-forward a few years: Sarah and Todd meet and fall madly in love. After a quick courtship, they decide to marry because they believe each is the other's soul mate. After the honeymoon, Sarah is in charging of paying their bills. She is careful with money and notices after they combine their checking accounts that their monthly expenses are significantly greater than she had anticipated. Todd spends money on things Sarah considers extravagant; he wants the top brands and latest technology. Todd waves his hand dismissively when she confronts him about spending. "I know it will all be just fine. Don't worry about it. You know I am good for it. Why do you have to come after me when I spend money I have earned? You are blowing this way out of proportion." Sarah's increasing agitation about money and apprehensions that maybe she can't trust Todd with money lead her to believe that perhaps she was even foolish to have trusted him at all. Todd is frustrated with Sarah's controlling behavior. Their fighting is escalating, and the distance in their relationship is growing. Something as simple as deciding what to eat for dinner can quickly turn into World War III. They come into our counseling office, each desperately hoping we can fix the other person.

Sarah and Todd need help learning how to unite against their money struggles instead of turning against each other. Both need to explore their strong emotional reactions to money and take down their walls to let their partner in. Sarah comes to understand that her fears of repeating her childhood experience with Todd cause her to be angry, defensive, and critical. In tears, Sarah shares her terror of her life falling apart without the security of financial stability. As Todd hears her pain, he reaches to his wife to offer comfort. He had no idea she was so scared and understands her reactions to money in a whole new, empathetic way.

However, this breakthrough isn't the end, as Todd also needs to appreciate the value of vulnerability. With help, Todd starts to see how his avoidance of financial responsibility really camouflages his own fears of inadequacy and his wife's disapproval. Todd shares the intense pressure he feels to please people and how buying things is the one way he feels like he is taking care of himself. As Todd lets Sarah into his vulnerability, she tells him she wants to help and take care of him. Sarah says, "You deserve someone to be with you in your struggle," and Todd's shoulders relax, his burden lightened.

The process of mutually responding to each other's needs is courageous and redemptive for both of them. Once they are able to be honest about their own stories and lovingly respond in that place of truth, then it is a lot easier to discuss budgeting and to find creative solutions to money problems. Free of emotional attachments, financial numbers are simply numbers. Todd and Sarah learned the value of transforming their distress into eustress, as the intimidating topic of money became their doorway into a deeper connection.

Having a partner to connect with over money really changes how the stress impacts us. The American Psychological Association's most recent report "Stress in America" shows on a 10-point scale (1 equals low stress, 10 equals high stress) that people who report having emotional support in their lives have an average score of 4.8, compared to 6.2 for those without any support.[11] A difference of 1.4 is statistically significant on a 10-point scale. As we noted earlier, this same report finds money to be the most common stressor in relationships. The plethora of research supporting the benefits of sound relationships in handling stress is beyond the scope of this book. However, we want to reiterate how all the research is supporting our simple message: the best way to deal with stress is to allow it to bring us closer to those we love.

Money and Spirituality

The first commandment in the Decalogue is, "You shall have no other gods before me," and unfortunately, many people's obsession with money turns it into an idol of worship. Jesus tells us we can't serve both money and God; we must choose one. The emphasis in many spiritual traditions on the importance of relationship over wealth often causes religious leaders to teach and preach that money is inherently evil, or at least the "root of all evil" (although the Bible verse alluded to, 1 Timothy 6:10, says, "The *love* of money is a root of all kinds of evil") in their efforts to protect the faithful from losing their way. Religious reservations about money arise from countless examples of how the addictive nature of money turns people away from God. We believe that God can use everything in life as material for glory. Money is no exception. If our hearts value God above all else, then money can be helpful in advancing what is good.

The Scriptures have many stories of how money was the impetus for transformation. In the Christian Scriptures, the poor widow demonstrates her healthy relationship with both God and money by donating all she has to live on for God's purposes. Her positive example highlights her conviction that money is just a passing object, while God's love has eternal value. According to inspirational author Rick Warren:

> There is only one antidote to materialism: generosity. Every time you're generous, you have a spiritual victory in your heart. Every time you're generous, your heart grows.... Choose generosity. It will transform your relationships with other people and your relationship with God. It will change you from the inside out as you learn to be generous like God is generous with you.[12]

Because the tax collector Zacchaeus encountered God's grace, he was able to acknowledge his sin and vulnerability concerning money and his life was redeemed. The Scriptures bear witness to many others who in their brokenness and powerlessness (often around financial status or standing) turned toward God for grace and forgiveness. In spite of their emotions of shame, guilt, and emptiness, encountering a loving God allowed them to replace the false idol of money with the goodness of a real relationship with God. After all, God came to seek and save the lost. Our longings and desires can be the doorway into hope and restoration.

Even when physical resources are scarce, we always possess the capacity to connect with another or our Creator. When we wake up to who we really are, we begin to realize that we are not here just to struggle and survive. We are here to love, create, expand, and thrive. Abundance and happiness are the by-products of the mutual dance of relationships.

CHAPTER 7

Claiming Strength and Resiliency

Overcoming the Wounds of Trauma

Our world has no shortage of bad things lurking in the shadows, including natural disasters, accidents, and human violations such as abuse, neglect, crime, war, and terrorism. While money is a daily stressor, trauma is an out-of-the-ordinary event that can instantly change our lives. Trauma is an unavoidable reality for many of us. Seventy percent of adults in the United States have experienced some type of traumatic event at least once in their lives.[1] Trauma is never something we choose to experience; rather, we find ourselves victims of circumstances that are outside us and out of our control, which can leave us feeling powerless. Trauma overwhelms our psyche and biology. We may freeze up, go into shock, and experience a sense of numbness as we try to make sense of that which seems senseless.

Sadly, often the traumatic event isn't the worst part. The worst is what follows afterward. Trauma results in constant preoccupation with avoiding danger and trauma triggers, such as people, places, and things that remind us of the event. This constant worry about the future makes staying in the present moment difficult. For many firefighters after 9/11, the worst part wasn't the towers collapsing, but actually trying to live in a new world of lost friends, constant media coverage, and fears of new attacks. Not knowing what is going to happen elicits massive amounts of anxiety and helplessness.

For children, outcomes of trauma are even more damaging. The Centers for Disease Control and Prevention and Kaiser Permanente collaborated on the Adverse Childhood Experiences (ACE) Study, which found that the higher number of traumatic events a child experiences (the higher a child's ACE scores), the worse her health outcomes, ranging from depression to cancer, heart disease, chronic obstructive pulmonary disease, and hepatitis. Adverse childhood experiences (ACEs) are defined as "physical, emotional, or sexual abuse; physical or emotional neglect; parental mental illness; substance dependence; incarceration; parental separation or divorce; or domestic violence."[2] These losses affect so many children that pediatrician Nadine Burke Harris considers ACEs "the single greatest unaddressed public health threat facing our nation today."[3] Without having the tools to cope or heal from childhood trauma, these children, as they age, will contend with serious, long-term health consequences.

A traumatic event can affect us regardless of age. It can happen to us firsthand or we can be witnesses to it. It may be a natural disaster or the result of human actions. It can also include the "unexpected death of a loved one, the loss of a job, a car accident, severe illness, hospitalization or surgery, divorce, bullying, a hostile work environment and living in a stressful psychosocial environment, as occurs in family systems in which domestic violence or alcoholism is present."[4] Most people in their lifetime sustain a number of these challenges. Some will come away from these experiences with unresolved trauma that continues to resurface and disrupt their lives and relationships. Some of us who experience traumatic events will develop a posttraumatic stress disorder (PTSD). PTSD can "occur after exposure to a single or repeated traumatic event that results in a significant emotional reaction involving intense fear, helplessness, horror or threat of serious bodily injury or death."[5]

We are just starting to realize the devastating consequences of trauma on so many levels. The amount of trauma we have experienced and how we have processed it can impact the outcomes for dealing with future traumas. The realities of trauma in the body and mind are seismic and measureable. Those with PTSD can have persistent states of chronic physiological hyperarousal, which negatively affect mood, increase inflammation, exhaust the immune system, disrupt digestion, and decrease the production of thyroid hormones that modulate metabolism and other systems of general regulation. The person experiences anxiety and fear, even when the environment is safe.[6]

When our body is activated in the way described, stress can significantly damage our ability to cope and function in responsible and healthy ways. Even more frightening, genetic changes caused by trauma can be passed down to our children, along with negative emotional patterns that we model. A traumatic event like the Holocaust doesn't just impact those affected but generations afterward.

How Trauma Intensifies Distress

When the brain experiences trauma, it adapts to better predict future situations and interpret new environments. The brain recognizes it almost died in the traumatic event, and it wants to ensure that doesn't happen again. Sometimes the severe stressors actually rewire brain circuits involved in the stress response, resulting in our getting stuck in a chronic fight-or-flight response. The amygdala, the part of our brain responsible for facing danger, takes over. Unfortunately, these changes in the brain often backfire, because the brain then perceives danger even in places that are relatively safe. Stuck in fear and hyperarousal, we fight at home with those we love because our reactive nervous systems overcompensate for threat and inadvertently push away the love we need to heal.[7]

To get away from the chronic threats and exhaustion of hyperarousal, most of us try to avoid triggers that remind us of the event, and the hallmark symptom of PTSD is avoidance. Avoidance is a great strategy for escaping overwhelming fear that seems to have no solution. After all, we can't go back in time and erase the event. Yet, when we try to outrun our fears, we find ourselves living in a very tiny world. After 9/11, many people avoided flying, going into large buildings, driving over bridges, or taking trains. I (George) remember every time I would see the NYC skyline driving into work, I would get a constriction in my chest and felt the urge to turn around. The tragedy of well-intended avoidance is it cuts us off from our own experience, disregarding our emotional signals while, as with hypervigilance, also keeping others out. As the walls close in, our fears increase, and so does our need to avoid. No wonder substance abuse, depression, and suicide are associated with PTSD. Too many traumatic-event survivors get stuck in a trauma trap where their attempts to avoid chronic fear results in isolation and increased insecurities about themselves and others, which intensifies the fears and need for avoidance. Trapped in the dark hole of trauma and hopelessness, it makes sense that any escape, including drugs or suicide, seems a viable solution to the unrelenting torment.

I (George) remember working with a family whose teenage daughter, Jenny, was sexually abused by someone in the extended family. She was "acting out" with a "bad attitude" and poor performance in school. Jenny tried to protect her family from the details of the trauma and believed it was best to fight her monsters alone. Hiding the pain of her dark side resulted in many secrets and mistrustful behaviors, which only reinforced her parents' concerns and criticisms. The following vignette demonstrates how the short-term coping solution of avoidance tends to exacerbate symptoms and family distress—and how risking vulnerability and openness creates connection.

Mom: I tried to be nice and prepare you a bowl of fresh strawberries, but all I get is your poor attitude.

Jenny: (*Looking away.*) I just didn't want them. What is the big deal? *You* always make a big deal out of everything.

Mom: (*Increasingly frustrated.*) *You* are always in a bad mood. It's hard to want to be around you. Nothing works with you.

Jenny: Now you know how I feel! Everything I do is wrong. I just want to be alone in my room.

George: It makes sense to get annoyed when you want to connect with Jenny and she doesn't respond. I guess I'm curious about what you were hoping would happen? ,

Mom: I just want to see her happy again. I miss her smile. (*Tearing up.*) She's got a beautiful smile, and it's gone.

George: Right, so under the anger is this sad place in you that really misses her smile? What do you think it would be like to tell her you miss her smile?

Mom: (*Pause, looking at Jenny.*) I so miss your smile. It's my fault you don't smile anymore. I'm so sorry, I let you down. I failed as a mom and let that monster rob your smile. I should have seen it. How was I so blind? How can you ever forgive me?

Jenny: (*Reaching over to hold her mom's hand.*) It's not your fault, Mom. I did a great job of hiding it. I didn't want you guys to hurt, so I figured I could keep it all inside. No one wants to know the details. Why cause you to hurt like me?

Mom: Please, Jenny, let me in. Give me something to do. I can handle it. We don't want you to be alone anymore. No one should be alone against so much fear.

Jenny: (*Silent, not making eye contact.*) I don't know. It's really hard. I hate myself for what happened. If I talk about it, it will only make things worse. (*Looking far away.*) OK, you want to know why I don't want fresh strawberries? That night when he first kissed me, he had just finished eating strawberry ice cream. I can still smell the strawberries, and I feel sick just thinking about it. (*Now sobbing, Jenny slowly rocks herself.*)

Mom: Oh, my God! (*Mom reaches over to hug Jenny.*) I'm so sorry! We'll never eat strawberries again! I love you so much. Thanks for telling me. We'll get through this. I'm here, my baby!

Jenny: *OK,* definitely no more strawberries!

Instead of perpetuating the old cycle of reactive blaming and defensiveness, Jenny and her mom started a new cycle of facing the trauma together. Taking full advantage of the extraordinary power of family love brings light into the darkness of fear and hopelessness and rescues us from isolation.

How to Think Differently about Trauma

Recognizing the good reasons we typically fall into the trauma trap of hypervigilance and avoidance empowers us to think about alternative strategies. The basic approach of any effective trauma treatment is to help the person to confront the very events and feelings he is trying to avoid. The best way out of trauma is to work through it. Regardless of the specific type of therapy, it all begins with the same first step: starting to talk about the scary event.

A few years ago, I (Heather) experienced the importance of confronting our traumas directly. My family was one of the many East Coast families evacuated from our home during Hurricane Sandy. Our neighborhood roads and lawns were underwater, and about twenty homes on our street and adjoining ones sustained significant flood damage. We tried to return and live in our home for a few days during the initial demolition of our first floor to remove walls and insulation now saturated with polluted waters. Our hope was to stay the course and continue living the way we did prior to Sandy. Soon, we realized we were the only ones left on the block. All the other families nearby had moved out and found apartments or were living with friends. They knew they needed to be elsewhere. I had blinders on that prevented me from seeing how bad things had become. I was avoiding the reality that we could no longer live in our home. I was afraid of the devastating financial impact of house repair and not being able to find a new place to live (many area apartments were already full with other displaced families). It felt like the wheels of my brain weren't turning properly, and I couldn't figure out what to do next.

What got my attention was my young daughter calling me during a work meeting and informing me she needed to leave school because she was wheezing. Although she had asthma, wheezing was not common for her, and I knew it was due to the mold in our home. One of my colleagues, hearing about my daughter, looked at me and said, "Heather, you are in shock." As a clinician, I thought I would have known if that was the case. However, I needed him to see it in me and speak the truth that I was too shaken to recognize. My psychologist friend gave me some simple instructions. They needed to be very basic for me to absorb them. "You need to go home, collect your daughter from school, get her medication, tell your spouse that it is time to pack your bags, and go to a safe place. Stay with extended family again, or go to a hotel, but you need to leave your flooded, mold-infested home. Get to a safe place tonight, and look in a mirror, and tell yourself over and over, 'I am safe.' Say it till you believe it." It was almost like he was talking to someone who was coming out of a deep sleep. I was groggy but heard him and obeyed. It was a life-saving moment for all my family. We had a number of contingency plans for the next ten months, but we survived, and I learned to appreciate the benefits of finding safety and confronting my trauma. Hurricane Sandy shook my sense of control and safety in the world, and I needed time to make sense of all the changes. My road toward recovery started when I put aside my avoidance and directly faced my fears.

Trauma is something negative to be feared, but in the wake of trauma, people often discover their strength and resiliency. Trauma can be the impetus for growth and transformation. Those with the courage to confront trauma often discover deeper purpose and meaning in their lives. Think about all the people who use the adversity of trauma to make the world a better place.

Changing our perspective on trauma empowers us to see ourselves and the trauma in new ways, setting us on a path toward healing and growth. To facilitate growth, we all must find ways to overcome fear and to replace fear with hope. Taking a more proactive approach that recognizes the positive potential of moving through trauma prepares us to feel less afraid and overwhelmed. If we are unaware of the positive potential, then we are susceptible to the ravages of trauma and will most likely resist treatment as we suffer alone. Thinking differently about trauma is the key to our ability to embrace whatever the outcomes are.

Embracing the Distress of Trauma

The good news is there is a clear pathway toward recovery and resiliency. Exciting new advances in neuroscience are shedding light onto how the brain heals after trauma. Talk therapy, a focus on gaining insight and solving problems to treat trauma, is inadequate because that approach is speaking to only a limited part of the brain, the thinking frontal cortex. Trauma is a significant event that involves all senses and affects the whole brain, especially the older regions associated with memory and emotions.

Psychotherapist Bruce Ecker's work on memory reconsolidation, recalling and recoding memories, provides a comprehensive account of how to heal trauma.[8] To begin with, the brain needs to be primed, actually tapping into the same state of consciousness as when the memory was encoded. This means if you were abused as a child, it is not enough to just share the information and facts. With a trained counselor, you actually need to return to the scene in your imagination—where it happened, what you were wearing, what you saw, how you felt, what you smelled, what you heard and said, and so forth. Focusing on the sensations brings the past alive and unlocks the synapses where the memory is stored. The key to rewiring the brain is that once the trauma is alive in the room, we attach a new experience to the opened synapses. When we add a new response of compassion to the trauma, that emotional experience recodes the neural pathways, changing how the memory is stored in the brain.

To attach new healing responses, we need to figure out what we need. One might think that knowing our needs would be easy and straightforward. Yet, avoiding our emotional signals to manage distress creates ambiguity and uncertainty concerning our needs. To unearth our needs, we must move toward our emotional signals. Listening to the emotion reveals our longings underneath. For instance, fear requires soothing, sadness wants comfort, anger needs to be listened to, helplessness longs for some control, and hopelessness desires some hope. Clarifying and communicating our needs is necessary to transform distress into eustress.

The worst part of trauma is the sense of disconnection from ourselves, family, friends, and God. Healing is found in a sense of wholeness or integrity and in experiencing deepened and honest relationships. The antidote to the chaos, isolation, and fragmentation of trauma is connection. While trauma colors the world as dangerous and floods us with fear and helplessness, connection offers comfort, soothing, and safety. While trauma creates overwhelming emotions that shatter a coherent sense of self and scrambles our ability to fully engage in the present moment, the connection of secure attachment promotes confidence in the self and others that enables the openness to fully experience what is happening in the present moment.[9] It is our firm conviction that distress that results from trauma is best addressed in the safety of healthy relationships. The power of connection, empathy, compassion, and love is delivered in many different ways. We can respond better to ourselves or invite in others—a friend, partner, child, stranger, or God. We are not created to face trauma alone. Listening to our emotional signals tells us what we need and pushes us toward connection, the natural remedy for the fear of trauma.

Partners excluded from trauma become additional sources of danger. Partners brought into trauma become part of the solution. The choice is up to each couple. To demonstrate what this process looks like, we will look at a couple I (George) worked with after 9/11. Rob, age forty, and

Marie, age thirty-eight, have been married for twelve years and have three children, ages ten, seven, and four. Rob, an officer in the New York City Fire Department, survived the collapse of the World Trade Center. Marie is an accountant who works part-time. Rob and Marie's typical marital problems were exacerbated by the distress of 9/11, and they began couples counseling in 2003 due to escalating fighting and threats of divorce. Prior to the couple's treatment, Rob had been diagnosed with PTSD and Marie with depression. Rob refused to talk about his 9/11 experience, as he believed Marie could never relate to it and didn't want to burden her with unnecessary worry. Marie felt disconnected, frustrated, and irrelevant. After five sessions of attempting to unite the couple against their distance and the negative pattern of Rob withdrawing and Marie pursuing, the couple started to feel more hopeful. I honored the good reasons why the couple avoided talking about 9/11 but also provided education about the costs of numbing and disengagement.

Rob:	I get frustrated just thinking about 9/11. It seems pointless to go back in time.[10]
George:	Right. Nothing can change the past so why bother. I guess my hope is if we can spend a few minutes going back to that day, then we can shed some light on all the good reasons for your nightmares and anxiety.
Rob:	Just thinking about 9/11 turns my stomach into knots. It kind of feels like it did right before the collapse. It's like, at some level, my stomach knew something bad was about to happen. (*Rob shakes his head and looks off into the distance.*)
George:	What is happening Rob? What are you seeing?
Rob:	S—t, what is that sound? Oh God, it's collapsing! (*Rob, experiencing a flashback, falls off his chair into the fetal position and tries to grab something on the side of his hip.*)
George:	(*Reaching down to rub Rob's shoulder and help him back into the seat.*) Rob, it's all right, you are safe here. You are here in my office. Take a deep breath.
Rob:	(*Trying to focus after disassociating.*) I'm sorry. (*Clearing his throat and shaking his head again.*) This is why I don't want to talk about it.

George: It always makes sense when we don't want to talk about it. Our bodies are trying to protect us. Rob, as you talked about hearing the building collapse, I noticed your hands were reaching for something. Do you know what it was?

Rob: (*Looking surprised.*) I just did that now? That is amazing. (*Rob closes his eyes and speaks.*) I was reaching for my radio; I had to let others know what was happening. Mayday, Mayday, Mayday.

George: So you were trying to reach out to others?

Rob: I guess so. That's why I don't want to talk about it. The whole thing reminds me of how powerless I am. Some of the greatest firemen in the world died that day. Good or bad, it made no difference. Who the hell wants to dwell on that? The whole thing sucks. It could have so easily been me. I have never seen such a sight. They never had a chance. I feel so bad for them. Losing everything. Never seeing their families again. So much twisted steel and smoke. I shouldn't be here today. (*Shaking his head with tears in his eyes.*)

George: Right. So much senseless loss and you feel you should have died with the others. Am I getting it right?

Rob: (*Shaking his head again.*) My stomach hurts. It is such a shame. I am the lucky one. I shouldn't be feeling bad. I have my family. I should be doing so much better. I don't know why I can't get rid of these memories. There must be something wrong with me.

George: So when you see images of the smoke and twisted steel, you feel like there is something wrong with you. You should be happy to be alive, but these bad feelings won't go away.

Rob: I never thought of it that way, but it seems right. I should have been stronger. (*Tears in eyes.*) I failed to measure up. It's not right to feel so bad. I'm disgracing their memories.

Marie: (*Reaches over to put arm around Rob.*) You didn't fail, honey. You did your best.

Rob: (*Pulling away.*) My best just isn't good enough. Everyone calls us heroes, but the only heroes died that day.

George: Right, so it is hard to trust Marie when she tries to reach to you and offer comfort?

Rob: I appreciate she is trying, but I don't want to hear I did a good job.

Marie: I'm sorry. I get it. You were just lucky to survive. It was scary and helpless. You feel there is something wrong with you because you can't be more thankful. I feel sad you were so alone. I don't know what to say, but I'm glad you told me. I love you, and I'm here whenever you need me. (*Marie reaches over to give Rob a hug, and this time he sinks into her embrace, crying tears of connection.*)

On a neurological level, Rob's brain changes with Marie's hug. The previous PTSD memory stuck at the moment of collapse and impending death is altered to include a corrective emotional experience of connection. Now, when Rob thinks about 9/11, attached is something positive that has emerged from the rubble. For the first time, Marie gets the volatility of his emotional swings and can offer her companionship for comfort. At the end of their last session of treatment, Marie said, "We always believed talking about 9/11 is too risky, like dropping a match into a tinder box. Now we know the truth: we can control the fire and actually use vulnerability to make us warm." Rob added, "I didn't think I could do the vulnerability thing and jump into my wife's dark hole without fixing it or let her into mine. Then I realized this is what I do with the guys at the firehouse every day. I unequivocally trust my fellow firefighters will do whatever it takes to come find me if I'm lost in dark places. We do vulnerability, we just don't use the word. I can do this with my wife." Couples like Rob and Marie, who approach trauma together, discover that teamwork makes them stronger.

A Spiritual Perspective on Trauma

The general understanding that trauma and suffering can be possible sources of positive change is thousands of years old. Christianity, Judaism, Islam, Buddhism, Hinduism, Confucianism, Taoism, and other religions all recognize the potentially transformative power of distress. Much philosophical inquiry, and the work of novelists, dramatists, and poets, has included attempts to understand and discover the meaning of human suffering.[11] Obviously, our message about the redemptive value of surviving struggle is nothing new. However, in our culture, which avoids the uncomfortable, this message needs repeating.

When spiritual writers from various traditions talk about contemplation of the divine, they describe this state of oneness with God as being grounded, at peace, where all the cares of the world, distractions, and demands fall away. Drawing close to God can be a way of being restored and filled. What a perfect picture those images conjure up as an antidote to the impact of trauma. Faithfulness can bring us back to our true self, our inner story, and also, deeper still, to the God story that we are invited to join. The ultimate good news is that in the wake of loss and destruction, there is potential for new life. All of life involves suffering. Coming to terms with loss and struggle can be a doorway to a more abundant and fuller life. Our perspective on what matters is clarified, and we can focus on what is essential.

In dealing with the stress of trauma, some practical spiritual practices can help survivors move into healing.

One method for reintegrating yourself when you get emotionally flooded with memories, anxiety, or sadness is to breathe deeply, hold your breath, and slowly exhale. (Interestingly enough, shortness of breath is associated with both depression and anxiety.) Repeat this practice four to ten times until you start to notice a change in your emotional response. Some people choose to associate words with their inhaling and exhaling, for example, breathing in life, God, or peace, breathing out fear, anger, or frustrations. Ruach Elohim, one of the Hebrew names for God, literally means "Spirit of God," but *ruach* can also mean "breath" or "wind." Our breathing is speaking "God," even if we don't know it. Our first moment, our last moment, and every moment in between include our breathing connection to the One whose name is beyond pronunciation.[12]

Another spiritual tool that many turn to for grounding support as they recover from trauma is prayer. Prayer is a way of tuning into and receiving the present moment and connecting with a source beyond ourselves. There are many different forms of prayer. For those interested, we encourage you to look into contemplative prayer, which with practice can help bring you back to yourself as you learn to rest in God's embrace. This form of prayer is about creating space to listen to God, rather than just to talk at God.

Often journaling about your inner story can be a way to restore your sense of self, to connect with God and sense God's movement in your life, and you can witness prayers taking shape in the process.

One other practice that can help anchor you in the storms of life and offer a new perspective is reading Scripture as a word of God spoken to you. In the Christian tradition, there is a practice of spiritual reading called *lectio divina*. A passage is read multiple times with silence in between to allow the words to go deeper and ultimately connect you to God in an even more meaningful way.

Being in the here and now, learning to breathe, praying, journaling, and reading Scripture are all survival skills that can expand our hearts and in the process turn the distressing challenges of trauma into eustress.

The Hebrew word *shalom* means peace but also wholeness, fullness, and completeness. In a sense, what people are striving for when it comes to repairing the disintegration of trauma is a reassembling or reintegration of that which has been broken. The mind, body, and soul need to come back online together for our whole being to find peace. In the Christian Scriptures, Jesus says, "I came that they may have life, and have it *abundantly*" (John 10:10). Another translation says "in its fullest possible way" (New International Reader's Version). We see life in the fullest as encompassing both joys and sorrows. It is accepting and embracing the challenges, trusting God can somehow make sense of the broken pieces and make them whole.

When life is hard, we are primed to learn something absolutely central. Trauma can be God's special hiding place. The place of the wound is often the place of the greatest gift.[13] The cross is necessary to experience the resurrection. Jesus took on wounds, faced trauma, to lead to others' salvation. To receive the gift of a full life, we need to be honest about our challenges and struggles. Being authentic with God, others, and ourselves is risky business, but it is also the movement toward connection, the path to safety, the way home.

Trauma to Eustress

At this point in the book, we hope our messages are getting predictable. Although we naturally try to avoid trauma, avoidance only works temporarily and inevitably leads to isolation. Avoiding fear pushes it underground, where it lurks and pops up unexpectedly. The more we hide, the more silence and fighting will take over our lives. If we fail to confront our traumas, they will continue to hijack our lives long after the event has passed. Redeeming trauma through the power of connection converts it into eustress, and that healing is transmitted to all those around us and even to future generations. The responsibility to find meaning in our trauma is something we must take seriously. So the next time you see your friend or spouse getting lost in his or her own world, or escaping into substances or technology, reach out a hand and invite him or her back into the real world of social encounters.[14] The connection enhances health and resiliency for both of you. Facing the trauma together changes the journey from isolated survival to mutual adventure and growth.

Befriending Stress

[We] should not try to avoid stress any more than [we] would shun food, love, or exercise.[1]
—*Hans Selye*

Whenever you face trials of any kind, consider it nothing but joy ... so that you may be mature and complete, lacking in nothing.
—*James 1:2–4*

The popular idea of stress as a "silent killer" teaches people to be afraid of stress and to believe stress management is their best survival tool. We want you to have a radical alternative to this limited definition of stress. We want you to be liberated and empowered to welcome stress as a friend. By destigmatizing words like *dependency* and *vulnerability* and restoring them to their rightful position of honor, we hope to unleash the power of stress to enrich our lives.

Stress is essential for successful living. Like a racehorse in training, stress allows us to stretch our strides farther and increase our galloping speed. Our lives can be so much healthier if we think positively about stress and use the vulnerability it creates to strengthen our relationships. Modern studies show that optimists have much better outcomes when it comes to dealing with stress.[2] Not reacting with fear allows us access to the best parts of ourselves—our creativity, passion, and unique gifts. Staying in the present moment is much easier when our brains are calm and we know the stress, no matter how bad, can be necessary and useful.

When we uncover the benefits of stress, even the worst events in life have redemptive value. Handling stress well is about resiliency, transforming adversity into growth. There are many things in life we cannot control, but that is not necessarily a negative. Our helplessness makes us need others. We may be taught otherwise, but being dependent is actually our natural, healthy state. The more comfortable we are with dependency, the simpler it is to turn distress into eustress. Interestingly, the more secure we are in relationships, the easier it is to be more independent when we need to be. At our best, we are both simultaneously present to ourselves and deliciously available to meet others' hearts.[3] Our clinical experience, scientific evidence, and much spiritual wisdom support the idea that our true nature is not based on survival of the fittest but survival of the most connected.

Emotional awareness and responsiveness are necessary to transforming stress. All of us can do it regardless of our circumstances. I (George) will never forget working with a Navy Seal who is great at his job. He is strong, smart, brave, and utterly calm in performing his duties. His background sheds insight into his ability to turn off his emotions. He grew up in foster care with plenty of abuse and no safe attachment figures. He learned early on the only person he can trust is himself. Joining the military as an adult, he advanced quickly, due in large part to his ability to emotionally detach and cognitively focus on the objective. His brief marriage ended due to distance, fighting, drinking, and infidelity. He never really received any emotional comfort and support. With a history like this, we might think he is destined for loneliness and isolation. But that urge for connection is innate, regardless of our experiences.

Certainly if we have never known emotional comfort, knowing how to receive it or give it is more challenging. Yet, when I asked this man to tell me about his five-year-old daughter he said, "She is amazing. I sit down next to her at bedtime and read her a story about how she is my princess and I'm her knight who will always protect her from the bad guys. I rub her hair and tell her how much I love her until she falls asleep. She knows I will do anything in the world for her." How does this man know how to perfectly provide his daughter the attuned emotional responsiveness he never received? The answer is simple: deep down this knowledge is in us all, part of our DNA. The universal nature of love is always looking to give and multiply.

Our Stories of Redemption
HEATHER

"Stress is cumulative," a therapist told me when my marriage was crumbling. I explained to her how I could not understand how our eleven-year marriage ended up in divorce, after we had been through so many trials together and been able to overcome them. We dealt with eight years of infertility, cofounded a graduate school with five other people, and moved many times. We each got a second master's degree and a doctorate after we were wed, dealt with the death of a parent, and finally had a wonderful daughter together.

At the time, the insight that "stress is cumulative" helped me make sense of it all. But while there may be some wisdom in that phrase, there is also a negativity and fatalism to it as well. As a result, I thought life must be about trying to avoid stress and thereby avoid the outcome that would be produced by too much stress. I became afraid and avoided stress. I now realize that stress does not have to be cumulative nor is it a death sentence for a marriage. There was much more of my story yet to be written.

Through grieving what was lost, being humbled by circumstances, receiving others' love and support, and finding a deeper walk with God through the losses, healing slowly emerged from the darkness. God didn't confirm my fears of brokenness. Rather, God showed me unconditional love. I began to trust that, regardless of my failures, in God's eyes I am worthy of love. As my heart expanded, I felt ready to risk again, and I met a wonderful man, Mark, who showed me that love is evergreen. His faithful pursuit of me and desire for my best, along with his strong intellect, kind heart, and great parenting skills, won me over.

That was seven years ago. We were married six years ago, bringing together a blended family of his sixteen- and nineteen-year-olds with my six-year-old. It was a new beginning for all of us. I cannot imagine my life without each of them in it and the fullness and joy they bring. We had a puppy join our ranks a year and a half ago, and to her, we are one big happy family. Despite the fact we have been through a flood and health crises together, I am so grateful that God does "make all things new." That renewal has been my story each step of the way.

One of the lessons I learned on the road to divorce recovery was about self-compassion and God's forgiveness. I realized how hard it is for me to be sympathetic to my own struggles. For many of us, extending grace to others comes naturally, but we don't treat ourselves the same way. Although I help people to work through a divorce or to get remarried, when I had to face the demise of my own marriage, it took years for me to reconcile with my new status. Self-compassion requires supernatural intervention. As the Twelve Steps of Alcoholics Anonymous teach us, a critical step is a reliance on a Higher Power. We need to recognize we are in need of a greater good than ourselves to change our lives.

Self-compassion also requires learning to forgive ourselves for not living up to the standards we held for ourselves or others' expectations of us. We are fallible and imperfect by nature. Yet, as many spiritual traditions would uphold, we are also made in God's image, endowed with a divine Creator who loves and intends us to be a blessing to the world. For me as a Christian minister, my faith tradition says that the brokenness and sin of the human condition is resolved in the person of Jesus Christ. He showed us the extent of God's love through God's intervention in human history, providing a model of love in the way he lived and died. Through his work, we have the solution to our shortcomings and struggles. Forgiveness is complete. In an unending loop, self-compassion is generated by a belief in God but also opens our hearts to receive God's love, which restores our sense of self.

In the process of writing this book, we (Heather and George) have come to appreciate the value of stress. Both of us have had to practice what we preach—reframing, listening to our own emotions, and living differently as we have confronted various stressful experiences during this season of writing. We have also come to understand that although stress can accumulate and can put a great deal of pressure on us, what matters most in our relationships with others and God is the strength of the bond between us and how we interpret the meaning of the stress. Close relationships with others—whether family, friends, or God—can uphold us and help us get through whatever suffering comes our way. Nurturing the bond among us and those around us is the best protection against the slow and insidious accumulation of distress. So let's raise our expectations. We can do much better than just surviving stress; we can thrive with stress.

GEORGE

Our egos don't like the truth that life comes out of death, but our souls totally understand.[4] The reality of redemption became real for me on September 11, 2001, the worst day of my life. If you had told me that something good could come out of that disaster right after it happened, I probably would have punched you in the face. There was nothing good to see, only tragedy and the horror of evil. God certainly seemed to "take the day off." Even now all these years afterward, just the mention of 9/11 elicits painful memories of twisted steel, choking dust, wicked smoke, jumpers, body parts, and the smell of death that doesn't come off your clothes or skin. So many negative experiences: reading through lists of those missing and hoping to not see the names of those you love. Nervously waiting for another attack as you see potential threats lurking everywhere. Delivering body parts to the ever-growing morgue, and watching search dogs get depressed because they can't find anyone alive. Working at the site every day with a chronic cough and knowing my health is permanently compromised. Spending endless days removing debris and yet the pile of debris never seems to go down. The nights were even worse as I helplessly sat with family members who will never see their loved one again. My head and heart hurting with so many unanswered questions, the endless funerals and constant bagpipe songs. As the days mounted, the darkness spread. I lost hope and longed for my life prior to 9/11. Despite my wishes, there was no going back.

There certainly were glimpses of hope in those dreary days: crowds of people cheering us on when our energy was depleted. The never-ending donations and food to keep our bodies going despite the exhaustion. The bucket brigades of helpers forming human chains to pass along debris and lighten the load. Solemn prayers at St. Paul's Chapel, the miraculous little church that survived the collapse, which offered a respite in the midst of the horrors of Ground Zero. The inspiring camaraderie of fellow firefighters and police officers upholding their proud traditions and creating a legacy for future generations to aspire to. The ceaseless support of family, and the unexpected appreciation from the world. Even though the firefighters didn't want the attention, they became symbols of resiliency and hope. Talk about irony. The world was applauding us precisely when we felt the most down.

As I mentioned in the prologue, my turning point came when I realized my pretense of strength was leading me into oblivion. Hiding behind a self-reliant appearance was a scared man whose world was upside down. My vulnerabilities and insecurities, which I considered a weakness, provided the components necessary for transforming my distress into growth. In the arms of my wife, I learned the power of connection to replace fears with hope. Our relationship soared as we faced our distress together. My previous conviction that needing help was surrender and a sign of failure shifted 180 degrees. Vulnerability does not need to be an exhausting, hidden burden. It is really a gift. I seized the truth that confronting and sharing our emotional signals is incredibly brave and offers us a pathway toward love and redemption. My broken heart mended through human connection.

To celebrate our victory over trauma together, I decided to put a bumper sticker on my car that read "I love my wife." It was a brave-heart moment, a way to express my growing commitment to vulnerability. The day I put it on, my brother said, "Are you crazy? You will not last a week with that on your car." I guess he knew something I didn't, as I drove away expecting no one to notice. After all, who reads bumper stickers? It turns out many people do, and I was amazed at the powerful responses this bumper sticker elicited. When I was driving on the highway, people would pull alongside and communicate all kinds of messages—honking, waving, smiling, cursing, giving the middle finger, and laughing. Pulling into the firehouse, I thought I would be safe, but the barrage continued. The guys let me know they wanted it off because they didn't want their wives seeing it and expecting them to do the same. The pranks were endless. For example, unbeknownst to me, my coworkers added new endings to the sticker so that it read, at different times, "I love my ex-wife, boyfriend, flowers, hot baths, your wife" and so on. The "I love your wife" brought a few extra honks of the horn.

It didn't make any sense, though. I could say "I hate my wife," and no one would say a word. Yet, when I publicly said, "I love my wife," everyone had a strong reaction. Parking at sporting events, I would always come out to see people gathered around my car, just waiting to see who would drive such a car. One time, I received a standing ovation from a group of women. Another time, I frustratingly discovered all the air out of my tires and a note that read: "Since you are filled with so much hot air loving your wife, use it to fill your tires." Part of me wanted to take off the sticker to avoid the embarrassment and attention, but to do so would have been to take a step backward toward avoidance. Vulnerability had proven itself to me, and I promised myself I was not backing down. I persevered and even received an extra fifty dollars when I sold the car. The dealer said, "This car will sell fast. People will buy it either to score brownie points or just to rip off that sticker."

As I got more comfortable with vulnerability, I started to look for ways to use my vulnerability to find more purpose and meaning. As I continued to work through my pain, I began to discover the treasure buried alongside the hurt. Stress isn't my enemy; it is my companion. Stress sets the stage for turning separateness into wholeness. Experiencing the benefits of facing stress with another person propelled me to help others do the same. The many places impacted by trauma that I responded to included NYC firehouses that had lost members in the line of duty; the Rockaways neighborhood in Queens, New York, after the crash of American Airlines Flight 587, which killed 260 people; Charleston, South Carolina, following the death of nine firefighters in a Sofa Super Store fire; Fort Hood, Texas, after a man on a shooting spree killed thirteen people; and New Orleans, following Hurricane Katrina. These experiences confirmed my growing belief that the worst of times bring out the best in people. I witnessed countless stories of people rising from the ashes of adversity. Trauma shatters the world, but gluing the broken pieces back together makes us stronger than ever.

Stress and Spirituality

As we have taken this journey together through the chapters of this book, our hope is that you are coming away with a deepened understanding of the meaning of stress and the hidden opportunities it provides. We trust the map we have provided showing you new ways of responding will aid you in engaging stress more constructively in your own life. We have discussed the value of reframing how we view a stressful event by listening to the helpful feedback our emotions provide regarding what we are going through, learning to handle stress, and, finally, learning to live life differently, engaging mind, heart, and soul. We have an opportunity to discover eustress in the moments when we initially felt only the weight of distress.

As many theologians write about finding the Holy in the ordinary, so too we can find the sacred in our stress. Many stress survivors encounter an experience of holiness in passing through a valley, whether that of illness, loss, or a myriad of sufferings. There are times in all our spiritual journeys when we experience uncertainty, doubt, questions, dryness, and even darkness. However, for many, a sustaining reality transcends even the ups and downs of relationship, the good days and the bad ones. Many of those who have journeyed farther on the path have a capacity to sense the Presence of God, even in what feels like God's absence. That capacity is paradoxical and transcends human understanding. But the Divine Presence is the one in whom they can find meaning, even in the cruelest and most unspeakable realities. Those with a connection to the transcendent, even in suffering, have found ways of seeing hope in the midst of despair.

For us, a sense of spiritual grounding brings freedom and power to make change possible in our lives. We know that our images of God impact our sense of self and security and, therefore, how we interpret stress. Many of us will find ourselves asking throughout our lives, "Who is God to me now? How do I see God?" So often our image of God is of a punitive parent, taskmaster, deity to be appeased, or cosmic Santa Claus whose list reveals who has been naughty and nice. For some, God set creation in motion but is an impassive, disengaged entity. The deep desires of the human heart reveal something of who God must be, however. The Christian philosopher Blaise Pascal observed: "Within each person is a God-shaped vacuum, only fillable by him." Where else might our longings for more than safety and nourishment come from?

We have found that a view of God as kind, loving, forgiving, and gracious will dramatically improve our view of self and our experience of others. We believe God's love is transformative. Viewing God as one who desires our best and calls us to participate in bettering the world grounds us and helps us grow. It gives us a sense of resilience, freedom, and strength to weather the challenges that life brings. We are not "alone" existentially, and we are empowered and loved by a source greater than ourselves.

As you consider your view of God or your own spiritual journey, do you find it liberating or limiting? In what ways does what you believe give you wings to fly? In what ways do your beliefs feel like a cage keeping you from all that life might have in store? Answering those questions will open up space for you to discover how stress can lead to the sacred. Difficult times often bring us to those existential questions and enable us to consider life and meaning from new vantage points that weren't open to us before.

Another important question many of us often ask is, "How does God see me?" What a miserable existence we would live if love were dependent on our getting it right and being perfect. Understanding God's view of us as "beloved" allows us to trust in God's responsiveness. Each of us—young, old, from different backgrounds, cultures, and times—desires to be known and loved. We are loved not for how well we perform or what we attain but just for being who we are. Ironically, the best way to increase our receptiveness and give everyone equal and universal access to love is to base it on vulnerability, not perfection. Love is actually easier to find in our struggles. When someone loves us in our failures, we learn that love is unconditional. Honestly using the pain of failure pulls people closer together and strengthens the bond in the process.

What might be different if we viewed God as an unconditionally loving Being who whispered to us in our lowest moments, "Don't fear, you are my beloved. I see you, know you, desire to bless you and be with you, even in this place that you find yourself"? Marianne Williamson, a spiritual teacher, author, and lecturer, described our calling as God's children:

> Our deepest fear is not that we are inadequate. Our deepest fear is that we are powerful beyond measure. It is our light, not our darkness that most frightens us. We ask ourselves, "Who am I to be brilliant, gorgeous, talented, and fabulous?" Actually, who are you *not* to be? You are a child of God. Your playing small does not serve the world. There is nothing enlightened about shrinking so that other people will not feel insecure around you. We are all meant to shine, as children do. We were born to make manifest the glory of God that is within us. It is not just in some of us; it is in everyone and as we let our own light shine, we unconsciously give others permission to do the same. As we are liberated from our own fear, our presence automatically liberates others.[5]

These words humble us. How dare any of us shrink back from being who God called us to be? We need to live full lives, not ones limited by distress, so that we can accomplish the unique role in the world we have been called to play. We are not designed to do it alone. God is with us wherever we go (Josh. 1:9 NLT).

Courage is required to change our image of God or ourselves. In our varied roles as counselors, chaplain, minister, and firefighter, we have been able to see what happens when people discover a sense of God's love and presence in their lives at critical moments. When we are really honest, which can feel raw and exposed, powerful things can happen. When we bring out our most shameful secrets or darkest fears, we find grace in another's listening and empathizing. When we are received by another without judgment, that reception calls forth our best and helps us accept and appreciate ourselves. Some people have responded with tears of relief and joy, and their perspective on their suffering has shifted. They are changed, set free from whatever prevented them from living with courage and hope. Wise religious traditions understand that spiritual growth is not only a path of ascent but also one of descent. Most of us believe in God's grace and mercy, but our plan for receiving it seems to be to never need it.[9] Focusing only on ascent destines us to hide and deny so many of life's inevitable failures, as if the only way to get to heaven was the way of perfect saints. That is tragic! God craves our truth, not our performance. God wants to meet us in both our highs and lows. Saint Julian of Norwich intimately understood how to encounter God and affirmed, "Our wounds are our very trophies."[10] Recognizing our wounds are the very things that allow us to encounter God makes these hurts incredibly valuable. Saint Francis of Assisi, when looking at the stars in his backyard, exclaimed, "If these are the creatures, what must the creator be like?"[6] God is magnificent, beyond comprehension, and capable of using everything, including distress, for God's eternal glory.

Ultimately, we believe God is connection and the loving space between all things. The love of connection is bigger than two people. It is a bond that belongs to neither alone, a fusion in which the self feels so permeable it doesn't matter whose body is whose.[7] God is right in the middle of a lover's embrace and parents cuddling their child. Love is the beginning, the middle, and the end, or as Jesuit priest Teilhard de Chardin wrote, "love is the source, the sustenance, and the goal."[8] Love is everywhere, and our receptiveness guarantees its constant expansion.

Looking backward over our lives often provides twenty-twenty clarity. Søren Kierkegaard observed, "It is perfectly true, as the philosophers say, that life must be understood backwards. But they forget the other proposition, that it must be lived forwards."[11] In the midst of our struggles, we (George and Heather) often felt lost, helpless, distressed, and cut off from God's presence. We protested, avoided, and made a mess of things. However, we got wise by making mistakes, not playing it safe. We learned to harness the power of vulnerability, and in doing so, we discovered God's fingerprints all over pivotal moments in our lives. Our parting wish for you comes from a powerful blessing found in the Christian Scriptures: "But for right now, trust steadily in God, hope unswervingly, love extravagantly" (1 Cor. 13:13, *The Message*). This beautiful blessing is available for all of us who embrace stress and faithfully acknowledge the eternal truth that it is our very neediness that ensures we stay in relationship with Love (God) itself.

Notes

Prologue

1. National Commission on Terrorist Attacks upon the United States, *The 9/11 Commission Report: The Final Report of the National Commission on Terrorist Attacks upon the United States* (New York: W. W. Norton, 2004), 311.
2. Daniel A. Hughes and Jonathan F. Baylin, *Brain-Based Parenting: The Neuroscience of Caregiving for Healthy Attachment* (New York: W. W. Norton, 2012).
3. Brené Brown, *Daring Greatly: How the Courage to be Vulnerable Transforms the Way We Live, Love, Parent, and Lead* (New York: Gotham Books, 2012).

Introduction

1. American Psychological Association, "Stress Effects on the Body," Psychology Help Center, www.apaorg/helpcenter/stress-body.aspx.
2. Meryl Davids Landau, "Hidden Risks of Chronic Stress," *US News & World Report*, September 18, 2012, http://health.usnews.com/health-news/articles /2012/09/18/hidden-risks-of-chronic-stress.
3. C. Liston, B. S. McEwen, and B. J. Casey, "Psychosocial Stress Reversibly Disrupts Prefrontal Processing and Attentional Control," *Proceedings of the National Academy of Sciences* 106 (2009): 912–17.
4. Hans Selye, *Stress without Distress* (Philadelphia: J. B. Lippincott, 1974).
5. R. M. Yerkes and J. D. Dodson, "The Relation of Strength of Stimulus to Rapidity of Habit-Formation," *Journal of Comparative and Neurological Psychology* 18, no. 5 (1908): 459–82.
6. Ibid.
7. Alan Zarembo, "Detailed Study Confirms High Suicide Rate among Veterans," *Los Angeles Times*, January 14, 2015, www.latimes.com/nation/la-na-veteran -suicide-20150115-story.html.

1. Reframing Thinking

1. Kelly McGonigal, "How to Make Stress Your Friend," filmed June 2013, TED video, 14:23, posted September 2013, www.ted.com/talks/kelly_mcgonigal _how_to_make_stress_your_friend.
2. Moshe Zeidner and Allen Hammer, "Coping with Missile Attack: Resources, Strategies, and Outcomes," *Journal of Personality* 11 (1992): 709–46.
3. J. P. Jamieson, W. B. Mendes, and M. Nock, "Improving Acute Stress Responses: The Power of Reappraisal," *Current Directions in Psychological Science* 22 (2013): 51–56.

4. Abraham Lincoln, *The Collected Works of Abraham Lincoln*, vol. 3, ed. Roy P. Basler (New Brunswick, NJ: Rutgers University Press, 1953), 81.

5. A. W. Brooks, "Get Excited: Reappraising Pre-performance Anxiety as Excitement," *Academy of Management Proceedings* 1 (2013): 10554.

6. "Law of Attraction (New Thought)," *Wikipedia*, https://en.wikipedia.org/wiki /Law_of_attraction_(New_Thought); S. Whittaker, "Secret Attraction," *Montreal Gazette*, May 12, 2007.

7. Daniel J. Siegel, *Brainstorm: The Power and Purpose of the Teenage Brain* (New York: Jeremy P. Tarcher/Penguin, 2013).

8. Richard Rohr, "Learning to See: Everything Is Holy," *Richard Rohr's Daily Meditation*, May 24, 2015.

2. Creating Connections

1. Gross, James J., *Handbook of Emotion Regulation* (New York: Guilford Press, 2007).

2. Ibid.

3. Brené Brown, *The Gifts of Imperfection: Let Go of Who You Think You're Supposed to Be and Embrace Who You Are* (Center City, MN: Hazelden, 2010).

4. Ibid.

5. Ibid.

6. Stern, D., *The Present Moment in Psychotherapy and Everyday Life* (New York: W.W. Norton, 2004), 76.

7. Brent Curtis and John Eldredge, *The Sacred Romance: Drawing Closer to the Heart of God* (Nashville, TN: Thomas Nelson, 1997).

8. Esther Perel, "Esther Perel on Mating in Captivity," interview by Lori Schwanbeck, 2012, www.psychotherapy.net/interview/esther-perel -mating-captivity.

9. Ibid.

10. Lynne McTaggart, *The Bond: Connecting Through the Space Between Us* (New York: Free Press, 2011).

11. Antonio R. Damasio, *The Feeling of What Happens: Body and Emotion in the Making of Consciousness* (New York: Harcourt Brace, 1999), 49.

12. G. W. Hansen, "The Emotions of Jesus and Why We Need to Experience Them," *Christianity Today* 41, no. 2 (February 3, 1997): 43–46.

3. Opening the Door to Transformation

1. See, for example, Paul Ekman, "The Argument and Evidence about Universals in Facial Expressions of Emotion" in *Handbook of Social Psychophysiology*, edited by H. Wagner and A. Manstead (Chichester, England: Wiley, 1989), 143–164.

2. Miriam Greenspan, *Healing through the Dark Emotions: The Wisdom of Grief, Fear, and Despair* (Boston: Shambhala, 2003), xiii.

3. Better Health Channel Contributors, "Anger and How It Affects People." www.betterhealth.vic.gov.au/bhcv2/bhcarticles.nsf/pages/Anger_how_it_affects _people, *Better Health Channel*.

4. Todd B. Kashdan and Robert Biswas-Diener, *The Upside of Your Dark Side: Why Being Your Whole Self—Not Just Your "Good" Self—Drives Success and Fulfillment* (New York: Hudson Street Press, 2014), 68.

5. Joann E. Rodgers, "Go Forth in Anger," *Psychology Today*, March 11, 2014.
6. Monica A. Frank, "Depression Is Not Sadness," *Excel at Life* (2010), www.excelatlife.com/articles/depression1.htm.
7. David Mrazek, "Sadness and Depression," *This Emotional Life*, www.pbs.org /thisemotionallife/blogs/sadness-and-depression.
8. Therese Borchard, "7 Good Reasons to Cry Your Eyes Out," *This Emotional Life*, www.pbs.org/thisemotionallife/blogs/7-good-reasons-cry-your-eyes-out.
9. Jerry Bergman, "The Miracle of Tears." *Creation* 15, no. 4 (September 1993): 16–18.
10. L. Bylsma, A. Vingerhoets, and J. Rottenberg, "When Is Crying Cathartic? An International Study," *Journal of Social and Clinical Psychology* 27, no. 10 (2008): 1165–87.
11. Alex Lickerman, "Turning Poison into Medicine, Redux," *Psychology Today* (2013), www.psychologytoday.com/blog/happiness-in-world/201301/turning -poison-medicine-redux.
12. "Fear," *Wikipedia*, https://en.wikipedia.org/wiki/Fear.
13. ADAA, "Facts and Statistics," Anxiety and Depression Association of America, www.adaa.org/about-adaa/press-room/facts-statistics.
14. Kashdan and Biswas-Diener, *The Upside of Your Dark Side*.
15. Ibid.
16. Brené Brown, *The Gifts of Imperfection: Let Go of Who You Think You're Supposed to Be and Embrace Who You Are* (Center City, MN: Hazelden, 2010).
17. David Shatz, Chaim Isaac Waxman, and Nathan J. Diament, eds., *Tikkun Olam: Social Responsibility in Jewish Thought and Law* (Lanham, MD: Rowman & Littlefield, 1997).
18. Albert Einstein to Carl Seelig, March 11, 1952 (AEA 39–013), in Alice Calaprice, ed., *The Expanded Quotable Einstein* (Princeton, NJ: Princeton University Press, 2000).
19. Ibid.
20. Todd B. Kashdan, *Curious? Discover the Missing Ingredient to a Fulfilling Life* (New York: William Morrow, 2009).
21. Martin Buber, *I and Thou* (New York: Scribner, 1958).
22. Barbara Fredrickson, *Positivity: Groundbreaking Research Reveals How to Embrace the Hidden Strength of Positive Emotions, Overcome Negativity, and Thrive* (New York: Crown, 2009).
23. Ibid.
24. Ibid.
25. J. Gruber, I. B. Mauss, and M. Tamir, "A Dark Side of Happiness? How, When, and Why Happiness Is Not Always Good," *Perspectives on Psychological Science* 6, no. 3 (2011): 222–33.
26. Kashdan and Biswas-Diener, *The Upside of Your Dark Side*.
27. Richard Rohr, *Immortal Diamond: The Search for Our True Self* (San Francisco: Jossey-Bass, 2013).
28. www.skylightpaths.com/page/product/978-1-59473-614-8.

4. Nurturing the Ultimate Connection

1. Y. Kim et al., "Quality of Life of Couples Dealing with Cancer: Dyadic and Individual Adjustment Among Breast and Prostate Cancer Survivors and Their Spousal Caregivers," *Annals of Behavioral Medicine: A Publication of the Society of Behavioral Medicine* 35, no. 2 (2008): 230–38.

2. R. Neumann and F. Strack, "'Mood Contagion': The Automatic Transfer of Mood Between Persons," *Journal of Personality and Social Psychology* 79, no. 2 (2000): 211–23.

3. J. M. Gottman and R. W. Levenson, "A Two-Factor Model for Predicting When a Couple Will Divorce: Exploratory Analyses Using 14-Year Longitudinal Data," *Family Process* 41, no. 1 (2002): 83–96.

4. The Gottman Institute, "Research FAQs," 2015, www.gottman.com/research /research-faqs.

5. Ibid.

6. S. M. Johnson et al., "Soothing the Threatened Brain: Leveraging Contact Comfort with Emotionally Focused Therapy," *PLOS ONE* 8, no. 11 (2013).

7. Daniel A. Hughes and Jonathan F. Baylin, *Brain-Based Parenting: The Neuroscience of Caregiving for Healthy Attachment* (New York: W. W. Norton, 2012).

8. Matthew D. Lieberman, *Social: Why Our Brains Are Wired to Connect* (New York: Crown, 2013).

9. Stuart Wolpert, "UCLA neuroscientist's book explains why social connection is as important as food and shelter," *UCLA Newsroom*, October 10, 2013, http:// newsroom.ucla.edu/releases/we-are-hard-wired-to-be-social-248746.

10. Kelly McGonigal, "How to Make Stress Your Friend," filmed June 2013, TED video, 14:23, posted September 2013, www.ted.com/talks/kelly _mcgonigal_how_to_make_stress_your_friend.

11. Ibid.

12. Richard Niolon, book review of *The Case for Marriage: Why Married People Are Happier, Healthier, and Better off Financially*, PsychPage, October 23, 2010, www.psychpage.com/family/brwaitgalligher.html.

13. Linda J. Waite and Maggie Gallagher, *The Case for Marriage: Why Married People Are Happier, Healthier, and Better Off Financially* (New York: Doubleday, 2000).

14. Timothy J. Keller and Kathy Keller, *The Meaning of Marriage: Facing the Complexities of Commitment with the Wisdom of God* (New York: Dutton, 2011).

15. Susan M. Johnson, *Hold Me Tight: Seven Conversations for a Lifetime of Love* (New York: Little, Brown, 2008).

16. Gershen Kaufman, *Shame, the Power of Caring* (Cambridge, MA: Schenkman, 1985).

17. Allan Pleaner, "Gottman Couples and Marital Therapy," CouplesTraining Institute.com, October 27, 2015, http://couplestraininginstitute.com/gottman -couples-and-marital-therapy.

18. L. Sobell, "Using Motivational Interviewing with Difficult Clients," keynote address at International Social Work Conference sponsored by University of Applied Services Northwestern Switzerland, Olten, Switzerland, June 13, 2013.

19. WebMD, "Surprising Health Benefits of Sex," MedicineNet.com, October 2015, www.medicinenet.com/sexual_health_pictures_slideshow/article.htm.

20. MSN, "More Sex, Less Stress," Mental Health on NBCNews.com, December 12, 2008, www.nbcnews.com/id/28146086/ns/health-mental_health/t/more-sex-less-stress.

21. E. O. Laumann, A. Paik, and R. C. Rosen, "Sexual Dysfunction in the United States: Prevalence and Predictors," *JAMA* 281, no. 6 (1999): 537–44.

22. iVillage, "The Good, the Bad, and the Dirty: The iVillage 2013 Married Sex Survey Results," Today Health & Wellness, July 30, 2014, www.today.com/health/ivillage-2013-married-sex-survey-results-1D80245229.

23. Kathleen Deveny, "We're Not in the Mood," *Newsweek*, June 29, 2003, www.newsweek.com/were-not-mood-138387.

24. Laura Silverstein, "What Porcupines Can Teach Us about Making Love," *The Gottman Relationship Blog*, February 18, 2015, www.gottmanblog.com/archives/2015/2/18/what-porcupines-can-teach-us-about-making-love.

25. Susan M. Johnson, *Love Sense: The Revolutionary New Science of Romantic Relationships* (Boston: Little, Brown, 2013).

26. William H. Masters, Virginia E. Johnson, and Robert C. Kolodny, *Masters and Johnson on Sex and Human Loving* (Boston: Little, Brown, 1986).

27. P. J. Kleinplatz et al., "The Components of Optimal Sexuality: A Portrait of Great Sex," *Canadian Journal of Human Sexuality* 18, no. 1–2 (2009): 1–13.

28. S. Johnson and D. Zuccarini, "Integrating Sex and Attachment in Emotionally Focused Couple Therapy," *Journal of Marital and Family Therapy* 36 (2010): 431–45.

29. Center for Sexual Health Promotion, Indiana University "Special Issue: Findings from the National Survey of Sexual Health and Behavior (NSSHB)," *Journal of Sexual Medicine* 7, Issue Supplement s5 (October 2010): 243–373.

30. Durex, "Best Sex Comes with Strings Attached, New Durex Survey Reveals," PR Newswire, April 3, 2013, www.prnewswire.com/news-releases/best-sex-comes-with-strings-attached-new-durex-survey-reveals-201237671.html.

31. G. E. Birnbaum et al., "When Sex Is More Than Just Sex: Attachment Orientations, Sexual Experience, and Relationship Quality," *Journal of Personality and Social Psychology* 91, no. 5 (2006): 929–43.

32. Markus MacGill, "Oxytocin: What Is It? What Does It Do?" *Medical News Today*, MediLexicon, Intl., September 21, 2015, www.medicalnewstoday.com/articles/275795.php.

33. Matt Fradd, "Three Things You Need to Know About Pornography," *Catholic Answers* blog, February 7, 2013, www.catholic.com/blog/matt-fradd/three-things-you-need-to-know-about-pornography.

34. See, for instance, www.marriageintimacy.com.

35. P. J. Kleinplatz et al., "The Components of Optimal Sexuality: A Portrait of Great Sex," *Canadian Journal of Human Sexuality* 18, nos. 1–2 (2009): 1–13.

36. John Paul II, *The Theology of the Body: Human Love in the Divine Plan* (Boston: Pauline Books & Media: 1997).

5. Enjoying the Wild Ride

1. *Parenthood*, directed by Lauren Neill (Orlando, FL: Human Relations Media Centre, 1989), film.
2. American Psychological Association, *Stress in America: Paying with our Health* (Washington, DC: American Psychological Association, 2015), www.apa.org/news/press/releases/stress/2014/stress-report.pdf.
3. Ibid.
4. Ibid.
5. Ibid.
6. Lisa Belkin, "David Code Says Parental Stress Makes Kids Sick," *Huffington Post*, November 4, 2011, www.huffingtonpost.com/2011/11/04/stressed-parents-sick-kids_n_1075317.html.
7. Robert M. Sapolsky, *Why Zebras Don't Get Ulcers: A Guide to Stress, Stress Related Diseases, and Coping* (New York: W. H. Freeman, 1994).
8. Kirby Deater-Deckard et al., "Conduct Problems, IQ, and Household Chaos: A Longitudinal Multi-Informant Study," *Journal of Child Psychology and Psychiatry* 50, no. 10 (2009): 1301–1308.
9. Sarah E. Romens et al., "Associations Between Early Life Stress and Gene Methylation in Children," *Child Development* 86, no. 1 (2015): 303–309.
10. Hank Pellissier, "Stress and Your Child's Brain," Great Kids!, www.greatschools.org/gk/articles/how-stress-affects-your-child.
11. Susan M. Johnson and Valerie E. Whiffen, *Attachment Processes in Couple and Family Therapy* (New York: Guilford Press, 2003), 58.
12. D. Howe, *Attachment across the Life Course* (London: Palgrave, 2011), https://en.wikipedia.org/wiki/Attachment_theory#cite_note-5.
13. Edward Tronick, *The Neurobehavioral and Social-Emotional Development of Infants and Children* (New York: W. W. Norton, 2007).
14. Workaholics Anonymous World Services Organization, *W.A. Book of Recovery* (Menlo Park: Workaholics Anonymous: 2005), www.workaholics-anonymous.org/2-uncategorised/37-affirmations
15. Susan C. Cloninger, *Theories of Personality: Understanding Persons*, 2nd ed. (Upper Saddle River, NJ: Prentice-Hall, 1996), 170.
16. Peggy Jones, *I Ching: Points of Balance and Cycle of Change* (London: Karnac Books, 2008), 129.
17. Conversation with therapist Precious Atchison in Seattle, Washington, 1998.
18. Robert Karen, "Becoming Attached," *The Atlantic*, February 1990.
19. Brené Brown, *Daring Greatly: How the Courage to Be Vulnerable Transforms the Way We Live, Love, Parent, and Lead* (New York: Gotham Books, 2012).
20. Gordon Neufeld, *Hold on to Your Kids: Why Parents Need to Matter More Than Peers* (New York: Ballantine Books, 2005).
21. D. Saleebey, "The Strengths Perspective in Social Work Practice: Extensions and Cautions," *Social Work* 41, no. 3 (1996): 297.

22. Parker J. Palmer, *The Courage to Teach: Exploring the Inner Landscape of a Teacher's Life* (San Francisco: Jossey-Bass, 2007).

23. Kenneth R. Ginsburg, *Building Resilience in Children and Teens: Giving Kids Roots and Wings* (Grove Village, IL: American Academy of Pediatrics, 2011), 22.

6. Breaking a Dependency

1. Oxfam, *Working for the Few: Political Capture and Economic Inequality* (Boston: Oxfam International, 2014), www.oxfam.org/files/bp-working-for-few-political -capture-economic-inequality-200114-en.pdf.

2. American Psychological Association, *Stress in America: Paying with Our Health* (Washington, DC: American Psychological Association 2015), www.apa.org /news/press/releases/stress/2014/stress-report.pdf.

3. Ibid., 2.

4. Brigid Schulte, "Why the U.S. Rating on the World Happiness Report Is Lower Than It Should Be—And How to Change It," *Washington Post,* May 11, 2015, www.washingtonpost.com/news/inspired-life/wp/2015/05/11/why-many -americans-are-unhappy-even-when-incomes-are-rising-and-how-we-can -change-that.

5. Daniel Kahneman and Angus Deaton, "High Income Improves Evaluation of Life But Not Emotional Well-Being," *Proceedings of the National Academy of Sciences of the United States of America* 107, no. 38 (2010): 16489–93.

6. Richard A. Easterlin et al., "The Happiness—Income Paradox Revisited," National Academy of Sciences, www.pubmedcentral.nih.gov/articlerender .fcgi?artid=3012515.

7. E. Diener and M. Seligman, "Beyond Money: Toward an Economy of Well-Being," *Psychological Science in the Public Interest* 5, no. 1 (2004): 2.

8. K. D. Vohs, N. L. Mead, and M. R. Goode, "The Psychological Consequences of Money," *Science* 314 (2006): 1154–56.

9. R. T. Howell et al., "Momentary Happiness: The Role of Psychological Need Satisfaction," *Journal of Happiness Studies* 1 (2011): 1–15.

10. J. Moll et al., "Human Fronto-Mesolimbic Networks Guide Decisions about Charitable Donation," *Proceedings of the National Academy of Sciences* 103, no. 42 (October 17, 2006): 15623–28.

11. American Psychological Association, *Stress in America Paying with Our Health* (Washington, DC: American Psychological Association, 2015), www.apa.org /news/press/releases/stress/2014/stress-report.pdf.

12. Rick Warren, "Which Will You Serve: God or Money?" Daily Hope with Rick Warren, June 4, 2015, http://rickwarren.org/devotional/english/which -will-you-serve-god-or-money.

7. Claiming Strength and Resiliency

1. PTSD United, "PTSD Statistics," 2013, www.ptsdunited.org/ptsd-statistics-2.

2. Nadine Burke Harris, "How Childhood Trauma Affects Health Across a Lifetime," filmed September 2014, TEDMED video, 15:50, viewed November 11, 2015, www.ted.com/talks/nadine_burke_harris_how_childhood _trauma_affects_health_across_a_lifetime?language=en.

3. Ibid.

4. Lori Russell-Chapin and Laura K. Jones, "Vulnerability and Resiliency to Life's Inevitable Trauma: Neurotherapy in the Treatment of PTSD," *Counseling Today,* October 2015, 20.

5. Ibid.

6. Ibid.

7. Jamie Kaufhold, "How to Recover from Trauma, Fear, and Emotional Blocks," *NeuroGym,* http://blog.myneurogym.com/evidence-based-redemption-from-trauma-fear-and-emotional-blocks.

8. Bruce Ecker, Robin Ticic, and Laurel Hulley, *Unlocking the Emotional Brain: Eliminating Symptoms at Their Roots Using Memory Reconsolidation* (New York: Routledge 2012).

9. Susan M. Johnson, *The Practice of Emotionally Focused Couple Therapy: Creating Connection* (New York: Brunner-Routledge 2004).

10. Transcript adapted from Susan M. Johnson and G. Faller, "Dancing with the Dragon: EFT with Couples Who Stand in Harm's Way," in J. Furrow, S. M. Johnson, and B. Bradley, eds., *The Emotionally Focused Therapist Training Set: The EFT Casebook* (New York: Brunner-Routledge, March 2011).

11. R. G. Tedeschi and L. G. Calhoun, "Posttraumatic Growth: Conceptual Foundations and Empirical Evidence," *Psychological Inquiry,* 15, no. 1 (2004): 1–18.

12. Arthur Waskow, "Why Yah/yhwh," *The Shalom Center,* April 14, 2004, https://theshalomcenter.org/content/why-yahyhwh.

13. Richard Rohr, "The Sacred Wound," *Richard Rohr's Daily Meditation,* October 16, 2015.

14. Barbara L. Fredrickson, "Your Phone vs. Your Heart," *New York Times,* March 23, 2013, www.nytimes.com/2013/03/24/opinion/sunday/your-phone-vs-your-heart.html?_r=0.

Epilogue

1. Hans Selye, *Newsweek,* March 31, 1958.

2. Valerie Maholmes, *Fostering Resilience and Well-Being in Children and Families in Poverty: Why Hope Still Matters* (Oxford, UK: Oxford University Press, 2014), 22.

3. John Amodeo, *Dancing with Fire: A Mindful Way to Loving Relationships* (Wheaton, IL: Quest Books, 2013).

4. Richard Rohr, "Losing Is Winning, " *Richard Rohr's Daily Meditation,* June 19, 2015,

5. Marianne Williamson, *A Return to Love: Reflections on the Principles of A Course in Miracles* (New York: Harper Collins, 1992), 190.

6. Richard Rohr, "An Evolving Cosmology," *Richard Rohr's Daily Meditation,* November 1, 2015.

7. Diane Ackerman, "The Brain on Love," *New York Times,* March 24, 2012, http://opinionator.blogs.nytimes.com/author/diane-ackerman.

8. Richard Rohr, "Learning to See: Everything Is Holy," *Richard Rohr's Daily Meditation,* May 30, 2015.

9. Richard Rohr, "The Power of Powerlessness," *Richard Rohr's Daily Meditation*, November 16, 2015.

10. Julian of Norwich, as quoted by Richard Rohr, in "The Power of Powerlessness," *Richard Rohr's Daily Meditation*, November 16, 2015, http://myemail.constant contact.com/Richard-Rohr-s-Meditation--The-Power-of-Powerlessness.html ?soid=1103098668616&aid=uT9DhPoJyig.

11. Søren Kierkegaard, *Journals IV A 164* (1843).

Suggestions for Further Reading

Amodeo, John. *Dancing with Fire: A Mindful Way to Loving Relationships*. Wheaton, IL: Quest Books, 2013.

Brown, Brené. *Daring Greatly: How the Courage to be Vulnerable Transforms the Way We Live, Love, Parent, and Lead*. New York: Gotham Books, 2012.

———*The Gifts of Imperfection: Let Go of Who You Think You're Supposed to Be and Embrace Who You Are*. Center City, MN: Hazelden, 2010.

Copeland-Payton, Nancy. *The Losses of our Lives: The Sacred Gifts of Renewal in Everyday Loss*. Woodstock, VT: SkyLight Paths, 2009.

Curtis, Brent, and John Eldredge. *The Sacred Romance: Drawing Closer to the Heart of God*. Nashville, TN: Thomas Nelson, 1997.

Greenspan, Miriam. *Healing through the Dark Emotions: The Wisdom of Grief, Fear, and Despair*. Boston: Shambhala, 2003.

Hughes, Daniel A., and Jonathan F. Baylin. *Brain-Based Parenting: The Neuroscience of Caregiving for Healthy Attachment*. New York: W. W. Norton, 2012.

John Paul II. *The Theology of the Body: Human Love in the Divine Plan*. Boston: Pauline Books & Media: 1997.

Johnson, Susan M. *Hold Me Tight: Seven Conversations for a Lifetime of Love*. New York: Little, Brown, 2008.

———. *Love Sense: The Revolutionary New Science of Romantic Relationships*. New York: Little, Brown, 2013.

Kashdan, Todd B., and Robert Biswas-Diener. *The Upside of Your Dark Side: Why Being Your Whole Self—Not Just Your "Good" Self—Drives Success and Fulfillment*. New York: Hudson Street Press, 2014.

Kaufman, Gershen. *Shame, the Power of Caring*. Cambridge, MA: Schenkman, 1985.

Lieberman, Matthew D. *Social: Why Our Brains Are Wired to Connect*. New York: Crown, 2013.

McTaggart, Lynne. *The Bond: Connecting Through the Space Between Us*. New York: Free Press, 2011.

Rohr, Richard. *Breathing Under Water: Spirituality and the Twelve Steps*. Cincinnati, OH: St. Anthony Messenger Press, 2011.

———. *Immortal Diamond: The Search for Our True Self*. San Francisco: Jossey-Bass, 2013.

———. *Yes, and ... Daily Meditations*. Cincinnati, OH: Franciscan Media, 2013.

Richard Rohr's daily meditations. Center for Action and Contemplation. https://cac.org/sign-up/.

Sapolsky, Robert M. *Why Zebras Don't Get Ulcers: A Guide to Stress, Stress Related Diseases, and Coping*. New York: W. H. Freeman, 1994.

Selye, Hans. *Stress without Distress*. Philadelphia: J. B. Lippincott, 1974.

Taylor, Terry. *A Spirituality for Brokenness: Discovering Your Deepest Self in Difficult Times*. Woodstock, VT: SkyLight Paths, 2009.

Printed in the USA
CPSIA information can be obtained
at www.ICGtesting.com
JSHW012034140824
68134JS00033B/3044